The questions for each day's dare will requi.. ... ...
and the impact of answering them is lasting. **The Respect Dare** *is not*
for the stagnant woman unwilling to grow or learn or change. **The**
Respect Dare *is not intended to create doormat wives, either. It's for*
the dynamic woman who, flawed as she may be, wants to love and be
loved.

~ **Krista Nunez**

Awesome book! **The Respect Dare** *contains a marvelous program for*
wives who want to learn what it means to respect their husbands and
to put their knowledge into action. The program works because it
encourages wives to move knowledge from their heads to their hearts
and behavior. The program is of benefit regardless of where you are in
your marriage (newlywed versus married a long time; happily married
versus struggling, etc.).

~ **Marilyn Johnson**

It's really encouraging to see God's faithfulness in renewing my heart
and marriage so quickly now that I'm allowing Him to lead. Our
husband's really need our respect, it's key for a man to feel respected,
especially by his wife. So grateful for Nina's insight and the "Daughter's
Stories" are so inspirational. Highly recommend **The Respect Dare** *for*
any wife, newlyweds or veteran wives!

~ **Brooke Byers**

As a disciple of wives struggling with troubled marriages, I took on **The**
Respect Dare *with great expectations. Because my husband of 26*
years is no longer with me, I chose to follow Isaiah 54:8, "For your
Maker is your husband – the Lord Almighty is His Name." What an
incredible experience, to do the dares with God as my husband!
Through this study I'm coming to know my God in more ways than I
could have believed or even imagined were possible.

~ **Patricia Evans**

When I married a disabled man, I was determined to improve his
quality of life by treating him as my husband and not as a patient. I
found a vital piece of instruction in Ephesians 5:33 where wives are
told to respect their husbands. **The Respect Dare** *helped me learn how*
by doing the daily dares. I wish you could see my husband then and
now. He has a new-found purpose in life!

~ **Sharon Cohen**

The Respect Dare

Published by Greater Impact Ministries, Inc. , 554 Belle Meade Farm Drive, Loveland, OH 45140

Scriptures are taken from the following: The Holy Bible, New International Version. Copyright © 1973, 1978, 1984, International Bible Society. Used by permission of Zondervan Bible Publishers. The Holy Bible, New Living Translation®. Copyright © 1996. Used by permission of Tyndale House Publishers, Inc., Wheaton, Illinois 60189. All rights reserved. The New American Standard Bible®. Copyright © 1960, 1962, 1963, 1968, 1971, 1972,1973,1975, 1995 by The Lockman Foundation. Used by permission. The King James Version of the Bible. Public domain. The New King James Version®. Copyright © 1982 by Thomas Nelson, Inc. Used by permission. All rights reserved. The Message by Eugene H. Peterson. Copyright © 1993, 1994, 1995, 1996, 2000, 2001, 2002. Used by permission of NavPress Publishing Group. All rights reserved.

Disclaimer: The names and details surrounding many of the stories have been changed to protect the identity of individuals. Any association with specific individuals is purely unintended.

Printed in the United States of America.

The Respect Dare

by Nina Roesner

For Jim...

the man I respect and admire
most on planet earth...

You are a great man and an excellent husband.

and in honor of the *Daughters of Sarah*®, who
actively live out Ephesians 5:33b, which reads,

And the wife shall respect her husband.

You are her daughters if you do what is right and
do not give way to fear.
1 Peter 3:6b

Acknowledgments

One cannot move forward in the presentation of this endeavor without first pausing to appreciate those who have contributed to its creation in the first place:

First and foremost, many thanks to God for His inspiration.

Thank you to my three children: Adam for creating the artwork; Bram for making dinner some nights so I could write and edit; and Elizabeth who nightly prayed for my hands.

A very special thank you to my best friend and husband, Jim Roesner, whose eye for excellence put the finishing touches on the book.

Mark Gungor, gifted speaker, pastor and author, who makes me laugh and wrote the foreword.

Greater Impact's Operations Director and my treasured friend, Debbie Hitchcock, who has an eye for both detail and excellence.

My dear friend, Barb Allen, whose grammatical skills helped me get it right!

Michelle Wittenbrook, Sharon Colvill, and Kim Conlin, who provided me with the confidence to proceed after reading it.

My friends, who encouraged me so very much along the way to persevere and finish the book. You are so precious to me!

And last, but definitely not least, the *"Daughters of Sarah"* class members who have lived and will continue to live the stories in the book. You are the story! You are beautiful in God's sight.

Foreword
by *Mark Gungor*

Scripture is clear on the difference between what men and women need from their mate. In Ephesians 5:33 Paul writes, "...(a man) must love his wife as he loves himself, and the wife must respect her husband." These words are much more than a command; they actually give us insight into the contrasting needs of a married couple. I am fairly certain that Paul wrote this advice because a woman's greatest need in a marriage is love, and a man's greatest need is respect. Clearly, believers needed a little bit of help to understand these concepts. That is why he was telling husbands and wives to do this. God was speaking through his apostle saying, "Listen up guys! You want to have a great marriage? This is what you need to do!"

Seems rather simple and straightforward, yet as I hear from countless couples every day, women are not feeling loved in their marriages and men are not feeling respected. Obviously, we are missing something.

Millions of people by now have seen the movie *Fireproof* where the couple in the film is struggling with this very issue. He does not feel his wife respects him, and she is not feeling the love from him. They are both miserable and their marriage is about to implode when the man's father offers up a challenge to complete a 40 day "love dare." The purpose of the dare is for the husband to show his wife he loves and values her. Each day's task or mission is not dependent on how she reacts or even accepts his acts of love and kindness.

In the end, the young man does win back his wife with consistent, unconditional love—even when it was not easy. He acted in love when he did not "feel" like it and even when his wife rebuffed and rejected his attempts and gave nothing in return. It is a fabulous lesson and a film I highly recommend to couples in struggling and miserable marriages. It is the best depiction I have ever seen of how one spouse can make an enormous difference simply by what they themselves do in the relationship. It truly takes one to heal a marriage.

The producers of the movie have even created *The Love Dare* book that you can read and use to do on your own for 40 days to improve your marriage. Now while the movie does a great job of showing the *love* part of it—and it can work the other way when a wife does this love dare to her husband—it is still more focused on showing love to your mate.

So when Nina Roesner contacted me and told me that in the same vein of thinking, she had written a book called *The Respect Dare*, I thought it was positively brilliant. Why not? If we can intentionally set about showing love to a woman, why not do the same with unconditionally respecting a man? Why not be proactive, sow into the relationship and give a man his greatest need rather than sitting around crying, complaining, and being miserable wishing for the other person to change?

We cannot change another person, the only one we can change is our self—our attitudes, perspectives, actions, and motivations. We need to stop praying, "God change my spouse," and start praying, "God change me." When we do that, when we die to our own selfish interests, find contentment in our relationship with God, let go of the expectations we have of the other person and concentrate on giving to them, an amazing thing happens. We become content and find out we no longer need our laundry list of demands met in order to be happy - and then the relationship grows and improves dramatically.

At one of my *Laugh Your Way to a Better Marriage* seminars, a woman came up to me and admitted that she had spent the first eight years of her marriage in a constant state of disappointment. Her husband (poor fellow) could *never* live up to all the expectations she had. Finally, she decided to sit down and write down all the expectations she had brought with her into the marriage. She said she filled out one page after another with all the ways she wanted to be treated by a man. After writing out every expectation she could think of, she put all of the pages in a shoebox, grabbed her husband's hand, and went into the backyard. She dug a hole with her husband and, together, they had a funeral for all those *unfulfilled* expectations. That night she changed her perspective on marriage. Her eyes lit up as she told me the funeral took place over twenty-five years ago and that she had been happy ever since.

This woman had learned a secret. She learned that it is not all about her, what she wanted and needed. She learned that she can be content in all circumstances and that her joy did not depend on what her husband did or did not do. What Nina has done in writing *The Respect Dare* is to show women how to get their eyes off themselves, off their own desires and needs, so they can learn to be focused on the most important relationship in their lives—the one with God. By doing this a woman becomes confident in who she is in Christ, she learns that her happiness is not about another human being, and she finds out that it is in giving that you actually end up getting so much more in return. Going through the 41 days of this dare will help every woman who accepts the challenge to become stronger, more self-assured, and able to fulfill the role God designed her for in marriage.

Most women have no problem with the idea of unconditional love and they need and expect if from their husbands. What so many wives have great difficulty understanding is that their husbands want and need to be respected just as much.

When a woman gives unconditional respect, she fills one of the most basic and important needs for a man. Respect is the oxygen that he requires in order to function, flourish, and be the best husband and person he can be. Respect is necessary even if he has not necessarily "earned it." Respect is a concept that many if not most women struggle with, but one that God certainly understands. He afforded men in the Bible great respect long before they were worthy of it.

Think of the story of Gideon. This quivering bowl of jell-o was hiding out in the cellar when God came to him and called him a mighty man of valor. He was acting anything but mighty! But God called Gideon what he was not, so he could become all he had the potential to be. In the end, Gideon ended up showing just who he really was and all that he was capable of when he triumphed in one of the most lopsided military battles in history.

Now consider Peter. Jesus called him "The Rock" long before he became a man of great faith and power, but was still mostly "paste and flour!" That is exactly what needs to happen in every marriage. Women need to affirm, encourage, and respect their husbands with their actions and words—and sometimes it is with the *lack* of words that is most powerful, if you catch my drift! Respect can be shown by what you say and often times by what you *don't* say.

Many times when I speak of this to women, they launch into 20 questions: What does respect mean? What does it look like? How do I show it? What if he doesn't deserve it? The list goes on and on. While there is no one-size-fits-all answer, or no recipe or steps to follow, understand that the concept of respect has more to do with *you* than it has to do with *him*.

I encourage all women to accept this respect challenge and find out if I am right. What do you have to lose except a whole lot of selfishness, bitterness, and unrealistic expectations? On the other hand, you have a great opportunity to gain greater understanding, self-confidence, joy, and a better relationship with God and your husband.

Go ahead, I *dare* you. You won't regret it.

Mark Gungor
Pastor of Celebration Church
Author of *Laugh Your Way to a Better Marriage*

Why This Book Was Written

Women get married with dreams, hopes, and aspirations of feeling fulfilled in the most intimate of human relationships, that of marriage. More than half end in divorce in the United States, and many women that stay married still suffer the same dismal death of their dreams. Captive within their own relationships and feeling inadequate in their ability to influence the world around them, women across America daily succumb in droves to despair, depression, and addictions.

Daughters of Sarah changes all of that. I started *Daughters of Sarah* as a non-denominational course for married women of faith, because I wasn't satisfied with the answers being provided to Christian women. I sat in workshops, read a myriad of books, and listened to speakers on the subject of a wife's role in marriage attempting to improve my own relationship with my husband. We are commanded in the Bible to be respectful and submissive wives. The treatment of these concepts in much of what I was reading and hearing was to place a woman in the role of a second-class citizen in her relationship with her husband. I continued to walk away with the perception that to honor God, I needed to give up the hopes and dreams I had and live out life as a diminished person.

For example, much of the advice dealt with not correcting one's husband or disagreeing with him. When I applied this advice, I found it frustrated both of us. Finally, I just started communicating more about what I was reading and asking his opinion. I found there is no formula for a happy marriage.

When I learned that, in the Bible, God described wives with the exact same word as He used for the Holy Spirit, I started to understand what God intended for His women that choose marriage. When I realized that God has given us all a spirit of power, love, and self-discipline, and not one of timidity (1 Timothy 1:9), I started experiencing the privilege of being a wife, as opposed to the drudgery of being one.

I wanted to do something for the plethora of women who loved God as I did, wanted to serve Him, and yet struggled with His Biblical instructions for wives as I did. I wanted to empower them in their relationships. I sensed that the 15 years I had been training other trainers and delivering training myself utilizing the most successful life-changing methods available were all for this purpose. I quit my job and *Daughters of Sarah* was born.

Tired of feeling alone in their marriages, and struggling in many of the same ways that I have, wives who participate in *Daughters of Sarah* emerge able to form life-changing connections with God, their husband, and their strengths. These wives emerge stronger, braver, and more effective in their relationships. Women caught in the quagmire of mediocrity - stagnant, unsatisfied, and wondering when their marital dreams for happiness and contentment evaporated - have emerged more confident, more capable at positively handling conflicts, as better communicators, and smiling at the days to come. *Daughters of Sarah* is an experiential training course like no other program in existence today that creates an environment through coaching, teaching, and accountability for real and lasting change to take place. Participant surveys done on this program demonstrate excellent results:

- 97% of graduates emerge more confident
- 95% improve their connection with God
- 93% improve their relationship with their husband
- Two full years later, over 93% say the results "stick!"

Having personally experienced this transformation within my own marriage as a result of applying the concept of respect to my relationship with my husband, I can attest to the value of listening to Ephesians 5:33b from the Bible, which reads, "And the wife shall respect her husband." I can still clearly remember those days of being frustrated, angry, disappointed, and primarily feeling alone and taken for granted. What is amazing is this transformation came not by my husband's actions, but by my own change in focus. Instead of paying attention to his inadequacies and perceived failures, I realized the truth that people can only really control their own behavior. When we focus on our behavior as we walk through our circumstances instead of emphasizing other people's failures and shortcomings, we can create changes that affect our relationships long-term.

As a professional speaker for women's groups and a facilitator of *Daughters of Sarah*, I have seen literally hundreds of people positively impacted by the understanding and application of the Biblical concept of respect. While all that goes on in a *Daughters of Sarah* course will not be experienced by reading this book, I believe and pray women everywhere can positively impact their marriages by understanding these Biblical principles and learning how to apply them.

Understand This First

If there were a way for you to greatly influence the state of your relationship with your husband, while growing spiritually, would you want to know about it? And more importantly, would you take action upon that knowledge? What if in 40 days, you could change how alone you feel? Or how much peace and joy you have in your life?

This is a book about what works. After listening to literally thousands of stories of struggles overcome and successes won from women in the *Daughters of Sarah* program, we have a great deal of evidence. A connection exists between the relationship a wife has with her God, her husband, and her strengths. This book is a glimpse into the lives of these women, what they have done to turn around their marriages, and what has taken them to the next level of relational intimacy. All the stories are based on true events. Their stories and the way their connection with God develops will affect you. The names and a few details have been changed to protect privacy, but the stories themselves actually happened.

What you will find in each dare is a verse, or quote, from the Bible, followed by a short story ("A 'Daughters' Story"), a few questions, and then maybe a prayer. We hope this format gives you a feel for some of the possibilities. We also want you to know that we do not feel that each story is the only way to act on that verse from the Bible. However, we hope that at the very least, some of the stories spur dialogue between you and your spouse. Our ultimate goal is increased healthy communication between the two of you. This will help you understand each other better.

We know that men are wired to interact with the world around them differently than women. Researchers have found that men's brains are physiologically different than women's brains. Men are beings where honor and respect matter greatly. Men often do things out of a deep sense of duty, even with the knowledge that it could be tremendously difficult or cost them their lives.

Remember 9/11? Three hundred and forty-three firefighters set their jaws, squared their shoulders, and began the one-hundred-story climb up the World Trade Center to their deaths. What goes through a man's mind that he actively chooses to walk into danger like that? As women, we will never fully appreciate nor understand this unique wiring, unless we learn to communicate and connect with the unique individual God created within our own man. Without this understanding, we are destined to live a life lonely and bereft of the intimacy for which we yearn in our marriages.

Congratulations for choosing to be brave as a wife, while embarking on this challenging journey with us. You are not alone - the voices and experiences of women who have walked it before you will guide and teach you as you follow some of their same steps of faith. This journey is not for the faint of heart, nor for those who are so self-reliant that they are unable to receive help from anyone. While it is good to be responsible and independent to a certain degree, we are relational and spiritual beings, created to co-exist in concert with others. It is our belief that *The Respect Dare* is something that will bless you immensely if you can persevere through what may end up feeling like a desert at times. Like Sarah in the Bible, who endured tremendous difficulty but was protected and rewarded, you are her daughters if you do what is right and do not give way to fear.

Are you ready to give an honest attempt to what works? Here are just a few simple rules to employ while we're together for the next 40 days...

1. <u>Take one day at a time</u>. Each day, start fresh, regardless of what has or has not happened the day before. Each day you will receive a new exercise or dare to complete. <u>You need to complete this exercise before moving on to the next day – if you don't do them in order, you'll miss out</u>. There is a necessary progression to the dares and the method has been proven – your results will not be as good if you don't follow the process!

2. <u>Have no expectations of your spouse's behavior</u> or you will experience discouragement and resentment. These negative feelings will always be born out of your expectations of your husband's behavior. Do not trust these feelings; they will eventually pass if you can continue to remind yourself to persevere. Your level of resentment and disappointment is directly related to how you are viewing your marriage – is this a context through which you expect personal happiness? Or are you willing to grow spiritually and use this context as a tool for that growth?

3. <u>Measure your progress in terms of spiritual growth.</u> Don't use the standard of our culture to evaluate your progress. We constantly compare ourselves to others and feel inadequate. Use only what you are learning about men, God, and the Bible to evaluate your growth.

4. Write your responses to the questions. Write down your answers each time we ask you to do so. This will provide you with clarity of thought and a needed perspective later. Sometimes you'll be asked to refer back to these writings, so be sure you have them!

5. Remember that this is a journey and that you will need to actively choose to take the high road, even when it seems pointless and without reward. Remember that sometimes action precedes feelings, and that our impulses cannot always be trusted, especially when it comes to walking the sacred ground in marriage.

6. Do the book with a few friends and meet once a week to encourage each other, if possible. What you are about to attempt is difficult. You will need support and encouragement to continue the journey. This walk is not for the faint of heart. Some women have begun this journey only to stop because they feel alone in trying to keep the momentum going. For those who need support, we strongly recommend the E-Course at http://www.greaterimpact.org . You will benefit tremendously from the interaction, coaching, perspective, and affirmation from both myself and fellow classmates. In addition to support while going through the dares, women receive additional video teaching that enhances the book experience as part of the E-Course. If you choose to do this with a group of ladies of your own creation, you have the option of doing the E-Course with a closed group. You may contact us via the website for more information. We also recommend the E-Course for the leader, and *The Respect Dare Small*

Group Leader's Guide. The guide takes your group through doing five "dares" a week for eight weeks in your church and provides excellent directions for a small group experience that deeply connects the women and builds confidence. It includes exercises that will make your small group experience unlike anything you have ever been through before. The guide is available from Amazon.com and other booksellers. Please know that the E-Course and Small Group Guide are significantly different experiences.

Above all else: Be of good cheer!

Many others have been down this path before you and overcome the same obstacles you will face. The ones that finish strong are those who are wise enough to know that growth is often challenging, sometimes riddled with tears, and often comes with a price to be paid – but the prize at the end is worth it. Know that most that have begun this journey finish it.

Dare 1
Expectations

☐ **Dare 1: Expectations**

You've noted you want to improve the state of your marriage and bring it into a place where it is a thing that honors and glorifies God. Even if your marriage is good, you can take it to a new level of greatness. There is always room for improvement.

What small tangible things would you expect to see changed in your marriage that would indicate progress was being made?

An example expectation for a wife that she would write for herself might be, "It's easier for me to refrain from telling my husband what to do or how to do things." Because we don't want to have expectations of our husband, we are going to write expectations from the past, then give them to God. An example of this one might be, "My husband rubs my back or gives me a hug nearly every day."

Write out three tangible, measurable statements that would indicate progress was being made for you, and three tangible, measurable statements that were expectations you have held for your husband. So you write a total of six expectations:

Expectations for My Progress:

1. _____
   _____
2. _____
   _____

3. _____

_____

Expectations I have had of my husband:

1. _____

_____

2. _____

_____

3. _____

_____

Please do NOT share these expectations with your spouse, but instead, tear out these pages with your expectations for your husband written on it, and place it in a sealed envelope. Put a date exactly six months from now on the envelope. Clip the envelope in the correct month on your calendar, and resist the temptation to think about it. Just continue moving forward in your learning about and application of respect for the next six months.

Pray the following now:

Heavenly Father, I know that I can lay my requests before you and then wait in expectation of Your provision (Psalm 5:3). My soul finds rest in You alone, and all my hope comes from You. Proverbs 16:3 tells me that if I commit whatever I do to You, then my plans will succeed. I claim that promise now, Lord, and ask you for this success in my marriage.

Make me like a tree planted by the water that sends out its roots by the stream and does not fear when heat comes. Its leaves are always green. It has no worries in a year of drought and never fails to bear fruit.

Father, I want to bear much fruit for your glory through the context of my marriage. Please help me do so as I cannot do it on my own! No one is like You, O Lord, majestic in holiness, awesome in glory, working wonders!

Father, I know that you have ordained me to stay in my marriage. My heart aches to feel loved by the man you have given me – and sometimes (or often) I do not. Please help me release these expectations to you, Lord. I eagerly await what you will teach me in the next six months – I look forward to growing and reflecting on that growth in the future.

I humbly dedicate my efforts to You my Lord, and pray that they are pleasing to You. Amen.

Thoughts Recorded for Today:

Dare 2
Introspection: Childhood

☐ **Dare 2: Introspection: Childhood**

Proverbs 9:10
The fear of the Lord is the beginning of wisdom, and knowledge of the Holy One is understanding.

All of us are affected by our childhoods and the example of marriage and family that our parents set for us. Much wisdom ensues from sifting through all of it, finding and implementing the "good stuff" and tossing out the "junk." We can choose whether to repeat the past or learn from it.

A Daughters Story...

Joyce recalled a time when she was eight years old, upstairs in her bedroom playing with Barbie dolls. She was wondering why it was so quiet in the house. Her dad was home from work and they had finished dinner not too long ago, but the familiar sounds – conversations, the TV, her parent's movements on the wood floor – they weren't there. She left her room, checking her parents' empty bedroom on the way, headed downstairs, and realized they weren't there either. She opened the back door, heading out to their detached garage. She froze in the doorway as she heard angry voices in the garage. She couldn't make out all that was being said, but she finally heard her mom say in a raised voice, "If you CARED, you'd show it – if I leave you, I'll take EVERYTHING, including your daughter!"

Joyce remembered being really scared and worrying that something bad was going to happen to her dad. The screen door to the house, which she had been holding open, slipped and slammed behind her. The voices quieted, the garage door opened, and out peered her mom. Her face was red and she looked really upset. "What do you need?" she asked her.

"I was wondering where you were," Joyce said.

"Go back in the house. Your dad and I are having a discussion," she replied.

"Are you mad?" Joyce asked her.

"GO BACK IN THE HOUSE!" her mom yelled. She turned and ran inside and spent the next several months wondering if her parents were planning to get a divorce, worrying that she might come home from school and her mom would be stealing her away from her father.

As Joyce grew up, this pattern repeated itself. Rarely did she see her parents have a disagreement, despite the frequent tension in the air – it was not to be discussed in front of her. But when conflict did come out in the open, it was an emotional affair, full of threats and shouting. As she got older, Joyce learned what it was like to be on the receiving end of this, particularly in her teenage years. Today, Joyce is 38, but the impact this situation has had on her marriage is simple – she never saw conflict resolved in a healthy way, and for years struggled with how to discuss difficult things with her own husband.

What about you? Be aware that your experience of your parents' marriage as a child has impacted the experiences, beliefs, and unconscious behaviors in your own marriage. Some of these beliefs are healthy, some are not. Sometimes our beliefs are not grounded in the Truth, but these beliefs still become the filter through which we see our own circumstances. An example of this might be a child who thinks he is the cause of his mom and dad's marital conflicts.

Today you will pray and ask for wisdom in understanding a key experience that has impacted the way you currently walk through marriage. After praying, wait for an incident to come to mind and work with it to answer the questions.

Lord God, it is my desire to make sense of my childhood experiences in a way that releases me from any inaccurate perceptions that color my current experience of marriage. Father, I ask that you bring to mind a specific incident from my childhood that taught me something about marriage – reveal to me Your perfect truth and show me any lies that I have chosen to believe as a result of that incident. Show me how this one event impacts how I currently interact with my husband. Release me from the falsehoods and reveal to me the truth. I pray for Your divine revelation and wisdom, my Lord.   Amen.

1) In one sentence, respond to the following questions: Who was there? When was this incident? Where were you?

2) What happened? If this is something that happened many times, just pick ONE of those times and describe it as best as you can, as if you were reliving that one moment in time.

3) What was revealed to you about how you interact in marriage as a result of this one incident?

4) What possible interpretations exist of that one event? For example, in the Daughters story, one possible interpretation of the event could be, "My negative feelings are to be hidden and denied to others." List as many as you can in seven minutes.

5) Write out a prayer of release for yourself from any unhealthy habits of thinking you've developed as a result of that incident.

Dear God,

Dare 3
Introspection: Biblical Wife

☐ Dare 3: Introspection: Biblical Wife

Jeremiah 17:10
I the LORD search the heart and examine the mind,
to reward a man according to his conduct, according
to what his deeds deserve.

Today, you will assess your current state, using a tool that
addresses various aspects of being a Biblical wife. We
want to clearly communicate that not all marriages are
created to be the same. What works in one woman's
marriage may not work in another. Whether or not we are
working moms may affect how our roles play out in our
homes, too. Thankfully, nowhere in the Bible does it say
that women are the only ones capable of doing laundry!
Some godly women manage their homes by encouraging
everyone to pitch in on the work, others hire services to
take care of housekeeping, and still others do all the work
themselves. We do not pretend to know what works best
in your marriage, nor do we prescribe a "one size fits all"
approach.

One woman may have a husband that really enjoys
cooking dinner and after a hard day at work, chooses to
unwind by preparing a meal for his family. Another may
be married to a husband that wants no part of that
particular task. Do you see how taking that away from the
first husband would be a negative, but a positive for the
second? One woman may be driving her child to private
school, another putting hers on the bus for public school,
and still another spending the day homeschooling. Still

others do not even have children. You will see as you go through the assessment that there are generalized terms used, rather than specific ones, in an effort to deal with the different experiences that people have.

One thing you will learn from this book and from the many stories from *Daughters of Sarah* is that what may work in one woman's marriage may not work in yours. Remember that the stories are merely examples of how one or two women chose to apply the concept of respect, and often times, that day's Scripture.

> The following assessment addresses aspects of what the Bible encourages for us as wives. As God searches our hearts and examines our minds, may we, with hearts desiring to be pleasing to Him, search as well. Prayerfully, but quickly, consider each and check those that are opportunities for your own development. Then please respond to the questions that follow.

Disciple

- ☐ Do I spend consistent time in prayer?
- ☐ Do I read the Bible frequently?
- ☐ Do I daily make decisions based on what I think would please God?
- ☐ Is my heart filled with gratitude for all God has done for me?
- ☐ Do I live my life for God or am I more concerned about what other people think?
- ☐ Am I more concerned with being holy or being happy?

Household Manager

- ☐ Are things "under control" at home (laundry, dishes, cleaning, etc.)?
- ☐ Is our home a relaxing and comfortable place for my family?
- ☐ Am I able to do what God calls me to do in my home without excessive stress related to its appearance?
- ☐ Am I comfortable when people come by unannounced?
- ☐ Am I well organized in my time management and do I comfortably and effectively handle multiple responsibilities?

Communicator

- ☐ Am I concise in my communication or do I ramble and go off on tangents?
- ☐ Am I considered a good listener?
- ☐ Do I speak the "language of respect" to my husband unconditionally?
- ☐ Does my husband confide in me?
- ☐ Do I handle disagreements well and yet get my point across without upsetting others?
- ☐ Am I critical or sarcastic when speaking to my husband?
- ☐ Do I ever criticize my husband in public?
- ☐ Do I often get emotional or judgmental when my husband opens up to me?
- ☐ Do I regularly point out things others do well?
- ☐ Do others perceive me as a positive person or a complainer?

Confident and Assured Woman

- ☐ Am I considered a confident person?
- ☐ Do people perceive me as arrogant or aggressive, timid or fearful?
- ☐ Do I feel courageous enough to do what God wants me to do?
- ☐ Do I have a spirit of power, love, and self-discipline, or do I have a spirit of fear and timidity?
- ☐ Do I worry about what the future will bring?
- ☐ Do I know God's purposes for my life and trust He will help me succeed?
- ☐ Am I confident initiating intimacy?
- ☐ Do I feel a need to manipulate others or am I confident?
- ☐ Do I handle life's challenges and problems gracefully?
- ☐ Does my husband have confidence in me?

1) How did you feel doing the evaluation?

2) Where do you think those feelings came from?

3) Can those feelings be trusted? Why or why not?

4) What are the two aspects from above that you feel most led to improve upon at this time? Why?

5) What would happen if you were able to grow significantly in those two aspects in the next 12 weeks?

6) What would that mean for your relationships with God and your husband?

Pray that God helps you see your way through to the growth He desires. Ask His help in making changes in your life. Ask God to equip you and grow you in the area of respectful communication with your husband.

Dear God,

Dare 4
The Vision

☐ **Dare 4: The Vision**

Jeremiah 29:11
For I know the plans I have for you," declares the LORD, "plans to prosper you and not to harm you, plans to give you hope and a future."

Isaiah 55:11-12
...so it is My Word that goes out from My mouth: It will not return to me empty, but will accomplish what I desire and achieve the purpose for which I sent it. You will go out in joy and be led forth in peace; the mountains and the hills will burst into song before you, and all the trees of the field will clap their hands.

Psalm 139:15-17
You watched me as I was being formed in utter seclusion, as I was woven together in the dark of the womb. You saw me before I was born. Every day of my life was recorded in your book. Every moment was laid out before a single day had passed. How precious are your thoughts about me, O God! They are innumerable!

Did you know God has a vision for YOUR life? He has specific purposes in mind that YOU were specially created to breathe life into for His people and His glory. If you are married, one of the purposes for your life is to become holy within the context of marriage, shining His light to the world.

Using the assessment you did on Dare 3, write a positive purpose statement in the present tense, describing how and who you intend to be in your marriage in four months. Use "I am" language, as opposed to; "I want to be," or "I will." Note the tense is current, as if it were already a reality.

Keep your statements as positive as possible, avoiding as many "I'm no longer (negative thing)," "I'm not," or "I don't" statements. Write about 200 words, being as descriptive as possible. Here's an example:

> *I am a woman of strength and dignity who holds her head up in challenging circumstances. I smile at the days to come and am confident, looking forward to what is coming my way. I am my husband's confidant, he entrusts his deepest cares and concerns to me. When I ask him if he feels respected by me, the answer is an enthusiastic, "Yes!" I am organized in my home and my children are able to find whatever they need because everything has a place and is in its place. I have peace in my home and am reliant upon the Lord alone for my happiness. I find my strength and my encouragement in God and spend intentional time with Him nearly every day.*

It doesn't matter if what you write is currently very far from the truth. What matters most is that you write a positive, present-tensed purpose statement of who you think God has planned for you to be and how you are to interact primarily in your marriage and family. Certainly one could spend time doing this in other areas of life, but for now, we will only focus on our marriage.

When you have finished writing your purpose statement, rewrite it as a prayer and tape it somewhere you will see it a minimum of once a day. **Begin the discipline of praying this statement as a daily prayer, from the heart, as you go through the remaining days of *The Respect Dare*.**

Purpose Statement Creation:

Prayer:

Dare 5
Me and My Big Mouth…

☐ **Dare 5: Me and My Big Mouth…**

James 1:19
My dear brothers, take note of this: Everyone should be quick to listen, slow to speak and slow to become angry.

Ever feel like God's timing for our husbands is a little different than ours? Moms seem to instinctively know things before anyone else. Even if we aren't mothers, there are still those times it takes our husbands a little longer to come to the same conclusion we have.

Wise women know that even if they might already have the right answer, they just need to be patient while they wait for God to teach their spouse. Whether you have children or not, you'll be able to identify with what Jan is going through in knowing the truth before her husband does.

A Daughters Story…

Jan sat across the table from her husband, finding her mind wandering from listening to Tim talk about his big project at work to worrying about her two girls, ages 2 and 5. They had dropped them at Tim's mom's house an hour before, and her mother-in-law seemed a little confused when they arrived. Having seen her several other times during the prior weeks, Jan noticed her confusion seemed to be worsening. She had concerns about leaving them there, and had asked Tim about it before they left home.

He insisted, however, the girls would be fine. So far nothing had happened and she thought she was probably being overly cautious.

As they sat in the restaurant, enjoying a quiet dinner to themselves, Tim's cell phone rang just as they were finishing dessert, and Jan could tell he was talking to their five year old. "What happened? Calm down and speak slower...Let me talk to Grandma. Mom, what's happened? What do you mean? I don't understand, can you just tell me what happened? Start at the beginning."

He became more and more frustrated, then finally calmed down as he was able to piece together the chain of events. He closed the phone and said, "My mother left a knife on the table and Joelle cut her finger. Apparently it bled a lot. We need to go get her and see if she needs stitches." They quickly paid the bill and rushed out.

It was a long enough drive to Tim's mom's house for Jan to conduct a pretty lengthy argument with herself. Sitting there watching the cars go by, she fumed. Hadn't she told him something like this would happen? She knew their girls weren't safe there. She was angry at him for not listening to her. Before she spoke, however, Jan remembered the verse she had committed to during *Daughters of Sarah.* Instead of being quick to voice her anger, she decided to be slow with it and attempt to listen, then see what happened.

After they had retrieved the girls and determined that the cut was not in need of stitches, she heard her husband say, "Jan, I am getting concerned about my mother. She seems a little more forgetful than she used to be and I think we should probably not leave her with the girls like this again.

I haven't wanted to admit that about her, but I can see now that you are right."

Jan could have taken that moment to give an "I told you so" lecture, but she also heard in his voice the pain of a son who was watching his mother age and change. She chose instead to simply agree with him and be thankful their girls were safe and sound in the back seat – and that God had taught Tim in HIS timing, not hers.

Bottom Line: Be quick to listen and slow to become angry. In this way, you can avoid an argument and stay out of God's way at the same time!

So What About You?

1) What potential disagreement(s) did you engage in recently that you could have avoided?

2) What compelled you to engage in the disagreement?

3) Sometimes just being aware of a Bible verse will show us things about ourselves that we didn't know before. What was illuminated for you today with regard to the verse?

4) Why does choosing to avoid an argument NOT automatically make you the proverbial "doormat," walked all over by others?

5) How can the verse from James impact your interactions?

Many times, more strength is required to respond with self-control than to react. Respectful communication often means not becoming emotional and arguing. If you think you disagree with your husband, try asking a gentle question instead to clarify or point out what information he might be missing. For this entire day, don't argue with your husband about anything he says, even if you think he is completely wrong. This is not an exercise in becoming a doormat, but rather an opportunity to discern how self-controlled you are. Pray for God's help in this.

Dear God,

Dare 6
Random Acts

☐ **Dare 6: Random Acts**

Philippians 2:14
Do everything without complaining or arguing.

As wives, we have a unique ability to impact and love those around us. The trouble is that we can often fall into the trap of feeling resentful if we do not receive appreciation for our efforts. If we are working full or part time, this can be especially challenging. One recent study confirmed that working women feel the primary responsibility for their housework, regardless of work status or pay.[1] Today's story helps us to think maturely while teaching us a very simple communication tool, namely that of stating the facts without embellishment or excessive emotion.

A Daughters Story...

Carol knew she had a lot to learn about expectations. Four days ago, she took Mike's shirts to the cleaners. This time she hung them in his closet instead of on the bedroom doorknob for him to put away, as she had for years. Carol even put them on plastic hangers, instead of leaving them in the bags on the wire ones. It was a small act of kindness, but she was pretty proud of herself, and expected him to notice. To her surprise, however, he didn't say one word to her about it. She was surprised and disappointed by his lack of response. Carol had managed to squeeze the chore into an already busy day, and fought rush hour traffic for twenty extra minutes on the way home from work so she could stop by the dry cleaners.

When she finally did get home, her arthritic hands were flaring up, and the additional work left them sore and stiff.

Tonight, when he came in for dinner, she was not as warm and welcoming as she had become over the last several weeks since working on applying respect in her marriage, and he did notice that! "What's the matter, Carol?" he asked, "You seem like you are upset about something."

She turned and stared, but she held her tongue. She was about to tell him about how she felt about the shirts and then it occurred to her that she would probably sound like their four-year-old grandchild when she starts whining. It's not like she was a young and immature wife – she was 54 years old! As she thought about it, she realized that to be upset because she didn't get a "thank you" for her effort was just that - immature. Mike was not even aware of the tough day she had when she picked up the shirts, and he was extremely stressed with his work too. She remembered her Bible verse for the week, "Do everything without complaining or arguing." She also remembered Who she was really serving. Carol thought of how Jesus poured His love on people who were considered totally unlovable in that culture; the sick, the disabled, the widows, the orphans, tax collectors, poor people and thieves. After all that Christ had done for them, and for her for that matter, she could certainly show a little sacrificial love to this average middle-aged man by taking care of a few shirts for him.

Carol made a healthy relationship decision. She decided to state the facts. "I picked your shirts up from the cleaners four days ago and hung them in your closet," she said.

Mike responded, "Yeah, I know. Thank you. And you put them on the other hangers. I appreciate you doing that for me."

Carol wanted her husband to grow in his faith, and wanted to model Christ for him, but she knew she was not going to have any impact by acting put out when she served him. That meant not getting all bent out of shape over a few shirts!

Bottom Line: Serve God and others will see Jesus!

So What About You?

1) What one act of kindness or chore can you do for your husband today?

2) How will your expectations (regarding your husband's response) be challenged when doing this?

3) Sometimes just being aware of a verse will show us things about ourselves that we didn't know before. What was illuminated for you with regard to today's verse?

4) Do you tend to state the facts, or do you communicate emotionally? What would be the outcome if you could communicate more factually in your relationship with your husband?

5) Why does choosing a good attitude while serving NOT make you a doormat?

True respect also means taking care of things that your spouse deems important to him. Today, while continuing to be quick to listen, slow to speak, and slow to become angry, do one act of kindness or a chore for your husband that you know is important to him. Actively choose to have a positive attitude and do this chore without expecting him to even notice, and without pointing out what you did for him.
Pray that one of the ways God will reveal Himself to your spouse (and others) would be by enabling you to love without expectation or resentment. Be certain to Thank God for any progress or positive changes you have experienced spiritually or relationally. This is the first step in living your life for the Audience of One.

Dear God,

Dare 7
If You Can't Say Something Nice…

☐ **Dare 7: If You Can't Say Something Nice…**

Ephesians 4:29
Do not let any unwholesome talk come out of your mouths, but only what is helpful for building others up according to their needs, that it may benefit those who listen.

Some of the friends we have in our lives really should be regarded with more caution. A good question for us to ask ourselves is, "Is my behavior influencing them or is their behavior influencing me?" We have the opportunity to be leaders in all of our relationships by whether or not we choose to be gossips, encouragers, or complainers.

A Daughters Story…

Denise met her two friends from her neighborhood, Megan and Leslie, one recent Saturday morning at a nearby coffee shop. They hadn't seen each other in a while, and as the women chatted around the table, the verse she had read that morning was fresh in her mind. It was as though she was seeing the both of them in a new light.

"I can't believe your husband still gets the newspaper in his boxer shorts! I saw him out there in all of his glory last Sunday," Megan exclaimed to Karen.

Leslie rolled her eyes. "Yeah, it's downright embarrassing. I thought for sure that getting that huge pair at the neighborhood Christmas party would have made him think twice about it, but I guess he's a slow learner. He certainly won't listen to me."

Megan leaned forward and said, "You know, I hate to tell you this, Karen, but it's not like I want to see Rob half-dressed, anyway." She quickly added, "Not that my husband Mark is any better of a physical specimen."

Leslie shook her head and chuckled, "I understand." Her eyes widened, "Hey, have you seen that guy that just moved into the house on Ridge Road? He goes running every day at about 5am. Now, there is someone I would love to see in his boxer shorts!"

They laughed together over that, but Denise thought, "How would Megan and Leslie's husbands feel if they heard this? It occurred to her at that moment this was one of the first times she wasn't joining in with them in the husband-bashing.

"Did you know Rob works out every night for over an hour," Leslie continued. "Not that it really does much good. You'd think by now maybe he could get rid of that gut. You should see him - he primps and preens like he's some kind of bodybuilder. Maybe his arms and legs are better, but ugh! He still needs to lose about 15 pounds!"

Denise thought it was great that he was making the effort to work out and stay in shape, but no one said anything about that. When she mentioned it, they both looked at her like she had three heads. Denise realized she needed to lower her expectations of these two women – to view their friendship in a different light. Lately, she found her attitude turning negative after spending time with them. She decided she could not have intimate female friendships with women who criticized their husbands, and were critical of about everything else for that matter. She would be careful not to speak about her husband in that regard, either. Whether her spouse was in her presence or not, Denise committed to respectful communication.

Bottom Line: If you are going to speak, at the very least be respectful, and you will impact your husband's reputation whether he is present or not!

So What About You?

1) How do you talk about your husband with your girlfriends, sister, or mother?

2) How do you think you are you doing in this area?

3) Are you feeling brave? Can you take a risk? Ask your husband if he ever feels diminished by you and the way you communicate with him. What happened? Write out what you asked and how he responded. Or if you chose to stay blind in this area, describe why.

4) Regarding question 3, is there a difference between what you thought and how he thought you were doing?

5) Pray for God to help you change in this area.

Dear God,

Many of our words tear down our spouse. We are not even aware of coming off as critical or disrespectful. In an effort to communicate respect today, only speak words that will encourage your husband, and refrain from communicating with him or about him in a way that diminishes him.

Dare 8
Remember…

☐ Dare 8: Remember…

Philippians 1:9-11
…that your love may abound still more and more in knowledge and all discernment, that you may approve the things that are excellent, that you may be sincere and without offense until the day of Christ, being filled with the fruits of righteousness which are by Jesus Christ, to the glory and praise of God.

So often we live in the moment and forget how far we've come. We do this by expecting our kids to be more mature than they are and by forgetting that our spouses are not perfect. Today's story depicts one woman's remembrance and recognition of what is still true, even though she long ago forgot.

A Daughters Story…

Crystal sat and looked at the questions for the assignment and drew a blank. Thirteen years had gone by and she literally couldn't remember why she had married her husband. Three children graced their lives and she and David were busy parenting, busy with work, and generally exhausted.

Pen in hand, she pondered the question, "What five attributes or strengths were reasons enough for you to marry your husband?" Thirteen years was a long time. "Intelligence," she thought, remembering the moments when he had impressed her with his business knowledge. "Good with kids," she wrote for number two. She smiled as she remembered the little boy in the apartment next to his that David would play with on Saturday mornings. "Passionate," became number three, as Crystal remembered their first kiss and the first few years of their marriage. She started to laugh, remembering how they could barely make it up the stairs to the bedroom before...well, anyway! "Adventurous," she wrote next, thinking of the long drives they took and how he never wanted to eat at the same restaurant twice. "Responsible," became number five. Crystal found herself smiling as she remembered her friend Joan's complaints this morning about her husband not paying the electric bill and their power being shut off.

Looking at the list, she realized that her husband was, for the most part, the same guy she married. Those strengths were still present in him; she just hadn't taken the time to recognize them recently. Her husband really was a good natured man, with good intentions. In thinking of some of her girlfriends, she realized she could have done much worse for a husband. She took a moment to thank God for the man He had given her.

Bottom Line: Wisdom comes from seeing the truth in the big picture and not allowing your perceptions to be clouded by life's daily challenges.

So What About You?

1) What five positive attributes or strengths were reasons enough for you to marry your husband in the first place? Write these down in list form, thinking back to when you were engaged and the first months of your marriage:

    a. _____

    b. _____

    c. _____

    d. _____

    e. _____

2) Why were each important to you at the time?

    a. _____
       _____

    b. _____
       _____

    c. _____
       _____

    d. _____
       _____

    e. _____
       _____

3) Ask God to show you recent examples of how your husband still possesses these strengths. What are you sensing right now?

4) When is the last time you communicated to your husband about his strengths? How did he respond?

5) How do you think your husband would react to you reminding him of his strengths every day?

Is your husband expecting kindness from you or criticism? When is the last time you really saw your husband the way God sees him?

Jesus died for him, too.

Why does God love your husband? As an extra challenge, when you are finished with the "remember" exercise, tell your husband what you wrote down and why, and then comment to him about how these strengths are still present in his character. Pray for God to show you these strengths and help you act on reinforcing them daily.

Dear God,

Dare 9
Project Overlook

☐ **Dare 9: Project Overlook**

Proverbs 12:16
A fool shows his annoyance at once, but a prudent man overlooks an insult.

Even if you do not live with a teenager, you might still be around them enough to understand their complexities. Teenage boys can be just as perplexing as teenage girls. These man-child creatures want all the benefits of adulthood while still frequently exhibiting childish behavior. It's tough to know when to treat him like the man he's becoming, and when to embrace the child he still is.

A Daughters Story...

Cami watched her fifteen-year-old stepson while he emptied the dishwasher. After two years of being a blended family, she still didn't sense a connection with this boy. "Do you want some help with those?" she asked him, in an effort to bridge the gap.

"Do you think I'll screw it up?" he curtly replied. She wondered yet again what she had done to cause the sarcastic retort. She decided not to react to his tone, but to try a different tactic. This boy was becoming a man. Perhaps the respect she paid her husband, which spoke volumes to him, would help her connect with this boy.

"No, Jacob, I just wanted to do something with you. I know you are busy this afternoon, so I thought I could just pitch in with you while you were here this morning."

He stopped with the silverware tray in his hand and just stared at her for a moment. "Seriously?" he asked.

"Yeah, you're going to the basketball game with the guys this afternoon, right?" she said, reaching out her hand for the tray. He gave it to her, said a single sentence about leaving in an hour, and they continued unloading the rest of the dishes together.

As she put away the silverware, she wondered to herself if she should attempt anything else. She decided to stay quiet and just finish the task.

"Thanks for the help," he said, as he closed the dishwasher and left the room. Cami smiled. She considered this a small victory, a small step in the right direction, and decided that her teenage stepson might be reachable after all.

After lunch, she got a glimpse of small progress in their relationship. "Hey, I'm leaving, I'll be back around four or five o'clock," she heard Jacob holler before the door slammed behind him. "Well, that's a first," she thought to herself, pleased in the knowledge that he had let her know when he'd be back.

Bottom Line: People (not just teenagers) are complicated. Extend grace and try different approaches when dealing with people and you will honor God in your relationships.

So What About You?

1) Prayerfully think of the last time someone insulted you, hurt your feelings or just responded shabbily. How did you respond?

2) How did your response help or hinder your relationship with the individual?

3) What have you learned from that interaction?

4) If you need to apologize to someone, please start by apologizing to God, then follow up with that individual. What do you need to do?

5) Are you typically someone who always overlooks an insult, or are you able to discern wisely when it is 'worth it' to engage in conflict?

6) Would others say you have a healthy way of dealing with conflict?

7) When and how does overlooking an insult prevent others from taking advantage of you?

8) Spend about fifteen minutes searching online or directly in your Bible the topic of God's anger. Make a list of what you find:

Remember that the Bible says, "In your anger, do not sin." It does not say to never be angry. Recognize there is frequently a difference between the things we deem worthy of anger, and those that God does.

Much of what makes us angry doesn't come close to measuring up to the righteous anger of God.

Today, think also of the compassion that Christ showed to the many people that were considered inferior in His culture. He healed the sick, ministered to the poor, and fed thousands. His best friends still didn't really understand who He was until He died and came back from the dead.

While being slow to anger, slow to speak, and quick to listen, actively choose to extend grace to your husband. If he says something that hurts your feelings or forgets something of importance to you, actively choose to not take something personally.

Pray that God will help you with this.

Dear God,

Dare 10
Good Advice

☐ **Dare 10: Good Advice**

Luke 6:37
Do not judge and you will not be judged. Do not condemn and you will not be condemned. Forgive and you will be forgiven.

We can be women of influence if we choose first to be good listeners and fully understand what our husband is telling us. The following story connects us to Nicole, a self-proclaimed 'former criticizer' who shows us one way to be a positive influence in her marriage.

A Daughters Story...

Nicole listened carefully as her husband described his work situation. He had been asked to lead a series of meetings, did not view the time investment as necessary, but his boss was really pushing him. He confided to his wife that he was uncomfortable with running these meetings and was tempted to find a way out of it. His boss had suggested a promotion may be on the horizon for him, but that he just needed to be seen by the senior staff more. "I just don't see the point in it all. Having meetings for 'exposure' makes no sense to me. Why would I waste everyone's time like that?" he asked.

"I can understand why you feel that way. I don't like to waste anyone's time, either. What did your boss say about inviting the senior staff to the meetings?" Nicole inquired.

"He said he wanted to promote me, but that he needed the executives to meet me, get to know me a little bit better, and see me in action. My work hardly comes into contact with their areas, so I don't why that matters."

Nicole smiled. Her husband, while brilliant as an architect and admired greatly by his peers for his technical abilities, wasted little time on office politics or promoting his achievements. She actually admired him for this, because he cared more for the work and the outcome of his projects than his own gain. At the same time, she also knew he stood under-rewarded for his talents because he didn't promote himself and didn't make the effort to play the networking game at the large company. She had also seen several people where she worked get passed over for promotions in lieu of other people who networked better. Nicole was aware that part of her job as her husband's wife was to be a "helper" to him, so she chose to be encouraging.

"I can understand why you feel that way," she began, "but I think you should do it. You're great at what you do. And your boss is probably right – he can do a better job selling a promotion if the people he has to sell it to have seen what he's seen in you. Even though you are uncomfortable with it, you know you are great at presentations and facilitating groups."

She looked at him and could see him chewing on what she had suggested. "I'll think about that. I never considered it that way," he said.

Three years ago, this conversation would have never even occurred. She would have been too busy interrupting him to criticize him or his boss. Nicole smiled at yet another benefit from respecting her husband that she saw active in her life.

Bottom Line: Do not judge, criticize, or condemn others, but instead be a woman who speaks carefully in wisdom and encourages her husband – you will find yourself more listened to and have a greater influence on those around you.

So What About You?

1) How often does your husband confide in you? Is it more or less than during your engagement period and first years of marriage?

2) When your husband tells you about his work situation, are you encouraging, or judgmental and critical? Ask him for feedback and just listen, do not justify any actions you've taken in the past. Write down what you learn.

3) When do you choose to give your husband advice? Is it frequent or is it only about important matters when he brings them up? How do YOU typically like to receive advice?

4) When you give advice, are you forceful and bossy, or are you gentle in suggestions? Do you use phrases like, "something you might consider," "an idea that might fit with that," "something others have found beneficial is…" or do you say things like, "Why can't you…" or "What you need to do is," or "I think you need to…"

5) What can you do to become a wife that is held in high esteem and respected by your husband as being a "safe" confidante?

Recognizing that most wives yearn for emotional intimacy with their husbands, it is truly amazing how so many of us miss the opportunities to create this by our own words.

A good listener knows when to speak.

Many times people just want to be heard, and not be given advice. Some of us have become people to whom no one listens because we are always offering suggestions, criticism, or judgment.

We think we are helping, but what we are communicating is an attitude of superiority over another person.

Today, be aware of your own advising nature. Your challenge today is two fold:
1) Resist the temptation to offer advice. Instead, evaluate the situation, perhaps asking the person if they want advice or want to talk.
2) Ask your husband if he considers you a safe person to talk with about his challenges. If he indicates you could stand to be better in that area, ask him how you can improve. Make him aware of your sincere desire to do so.

Pray for guidance, wisdom, and for His help in becoming the woman God desires you to be.

Dear God,

Dare 11
Whatever We Pay Attention to Grows!

Dare 11: Whatever We Pay Attention to Grows!

Philippians 4:8
Finally brothers, whatever is true, whatever is noble, whatever is right, whatever is pure, whatever is lovely, whatever is admirable – if anything is excellent or praiseworthy – think about such things.

Just as a child who craves attention will seek to garner this attention through any behavior necessary, good or bad, whatever we give attention to will increase in frequency. If we want to increase responsible behavior or kindness, we need to acknowledge those character traits when they emerge. Too often we only pay attention to the negatives. Is it surprising then if negativity begins to permeate our relationships?

Frequently we also manage our interactions with our spouse with an expectation that he can read our mind. Men are human, too. We need to remember that we forget things as well.

A Daughters Story...

Maggie sat in the garage and fumed with irritation. Three days ago she asked her husband to drill the holes in the wood planks so she could finish her projects for the craft show the next weekend. There they sat, untouched, on his work table. As it stood now, several late nights faced her so she could still participate and not lose her booth reservation fee. "Three times I've asked him to do these –

it takes him 15 minutes...why won't he help me?!" Her eyes welled with tears as she became angrier. As she walked from the workshop to the house, she remembered several weeks ago, when she asked for his help and he completely ignored her, not even answering. Instead, she took them over to a friend's house, and her friend's husband ended up drilling them for her. This time, however, when Brett saw her getting ready for the next show, he volunteered his time to help her. "I guess that's something," Maggie thought to herself, "It's more than he's done before."

Her verse, Philippians 4:8, flowed through her mind as she walked into the house and found her husband paying bills at his desk. "Brett, I really appreciate your offering to help me drill the holes this time for the craft show. Do you have time right now to do them? I'm behind in assembling the wall hangings and I'm worried about not getting them done if I don't spend time on them today. I can't do anything else until the holes are done."

Her husband looked up at her and replied, "Yeah, I can do that. Let me finish this bill and I'll be right out." She waited next to him and they walked out to the workshop together. Fifteen minutes later, he was on his way back to the house and she was thankful she had chosen to pay attention to what was true, right, and admirable instead of nagging or complaining to him about being insensitive.

Bottom Line: Think about what is right, pure, admirable, true, excellent, praiseworthy, and noble – and it will change your attitude and make you more successful in the way you communicate with others!

So What About You?

1) Please list several "achievements" from your life. These are things you have worked hard to accomplish, over time, and have (whether known to you at the time or not) received God's help in accomplishing them. Some examples might include finishing your degree after having kids, training an assistance animal, starting a Bible study in your neighborhood, raising a child, finishing your first quilt, etc. If you have difficulty in coming up with 3 of them, ask your husband, a sister, a good friend, and God for direction on which 3 you should pick from your life and list them here:

    1. _____
    2. _____
    3. _____

2) Prayerfully consider each of the above achievements. Which one do you sense God was most involved in for you? How?

3) Fully remember the details surrounding all the aspects of this achievement. Prayerfully make some notes about what was most important during this time. Think in terms of how you thought about challenges you faced, how you overcame them, what your thought patterns were like, etc.

4) What do you sense God wants you to know about yourself, based upon this achievement?

5) What do you sense God wants you to know about Him, based upon this achievement?

6) What do you sense now that you didn't know when you were in the midst of the achievement?

7) In terms of achievement, how are you viewing your progress in doing *The Respect Dare*? Go back to the "Understand This First" section at the beginning of the book and evaluate how you are doing in each of those areas. Do you need to make any adjustments? If you are in a small group, how is your group doing?

Whatever we pay attention to grows.

God tells us in Philippians 4:8 what we are to think about. If our thoughts are constantly focusing on those things, we are living life through the lens of the Holy Spirit. In other words, we can see life and people the way God does.

We can then pay an honest compliment before offering constructive feedback. We can also see how inaccurate our perceptions are. We can also build up others instead of tearing them down, all the while saying what needs to be said in a way that motivates and is heard. We need to use our negative emotions as cues to seek God's perspective. We can then sin less, and glorify Him more.

Your challenge today is to simply pray for God to enable you to see life through the lens of the Holy Spirit, to give you the ability to see what is: true, noble, right, pure, lovely, admirable, excellent, or praiseworthy – in every situation – especially those that cause you to be angry, hurt, or irritated.

Pray for His strength to accomplish this.

Dear God,

Dare 12
Leftovers

☐ **Dare 12: Leftovers**

Proverbs 31:26
She opens her mouth in wisdom; and the teaching of kindness is on her tongue.

How often do we make life all about ME? We forget that other people work hard, are tired or sick or simply are as busy as we are. Today we learn a little bit about perspective.

A Daughters Story...

Lisa found herself staring at the dinner dishes on the table after the end of an exhausting day of running kids to and from school, a doctor's appointment, and soccer practice. On top of all that, she had also worked six hours at her part time job. Adding stress to an already chaotic day, her husband called, needing her to run papers to a client 45 minutes away. Cheerfully she helped him out, but by the end of dinner, she just wanted to go to bed. Achy and uncomfortable from her period as well as depleted from the day, she asked Tim if he would mind taking care of the dishes and getting the kids to bed so she could take a bath and turn in. "Of course," he said, and off she went.

When the alarm went off at 6:00 am, Lisa wandered downstairs to start the coffee and was greeted by half of last night's chicken casserole still sitting on the counter next to the aluminum foil. Immediately, she was awake and irritated. "How could he forget to put this away last night?" she thought. "Do I have to do everything myself? Why can't someone take care of me without it costing me something?" She put away the aluminum foil and started shoving the remains down the garbage disposal. "After the day I had yesterday, it's no small miracle dinner even happened," Lisa fumed as she watched the last of the casserole disappear down the sink.

The drone of the garbage disposal gone, she heard her husband's slippers scraping the hardwood floors as he walked to witness her putting the casserole dish into the dishwasher. "Oh, gosh, I'm really sorry – I was so tired myself last night that by the time I was done getting kids to bed, I completely forgot I wasn't finished in the kitchen. That was a really good meal, hon'. I'm sorry I wasted the leftovers," he sighed.

Lisa looked up at him, sensing her Bible verse for the week flowing through her head. She opened her mouth and the words that came out resembled none of the emotion she felt just a few moments earlier. "You had a really tough day yesterday, too, I remember," she stated, almost as much to herself as to him. "I was glad to help. Don't feel bad about the casserole. Thanks for putting the kids to bed and cleaning up so I could relax. I bet you wanted to do the same thing."

Bottom Line: Sometimes an insult or injury is simply the actions of someone who is tired, just like we are. Be kind and you will foster that environment in your home!

So What About You?

1) Could you relate to the Daughters story? Why or why not?

2) Think over the last few days of interactions at the end of the day. How kind have you been? Have you been wise in your communication?

3) What can you do today to honor God in the way you speak to your husband or kids?

4) When you are tired, or drained, are you still able to empathize with others and understand if they are in a similar situation? Or does it become "all about you?"

Today, choose only to speak words that are kind. Choose not to say anything at all if you do not know how to say it kindly. This may feel at first as though you are letting others take advantage of you, but realize that instead, it is actually an exercise in self-control.   First comes the control, then comes the ability to see things how God sees them, then comes the ability to say things wisely to others.

Pray that God helps you keep your words wise and kind today and in the future days of this journey.

Dear God,

Dare 13
The Play Set

☐ **Dare 13: The Play Set**

Proverbs 31:27
She watches over the affairs of her household and does not eat the bread of idleness.

If we stay home full time with our kids, they are watching nearly everything that we do. While we can never be perfect, we certainly have plenty of opportunities to get it right and demonstrate that Mom and Dad are on the same team. Don't miss an opportunity to communicate what a good marriage looks like to the next generation.

A Daughters Story...

Meagan sat on the couch and sighed. Of all days for her husband to call from work and ask her to do something for him! And painting was not her favorite household task by any stretch of the imagination.   Exhaustion pulled at her limbs, and she found herself reclined on the couch, watching her two oldest boys, ages four and six, build a block tower while Meagan and Greg's two year old son finally napped for the afternoon.   "I'll just put my feet up here for a few moments," she thought.

The radio played in the background as she rested. "70% chance of rain tomorrow and Friday," the weatherman reported. "Ugh, if I don't paint the play set today like Greg wants, it will be the weekend before we get to it," she thought, remembering the company and plans they had already.

She remembered the verse she committed to applying and she felt herself listening and sensing a desire to do the right thing. "Okay, guys, let's take it outside," she coached the boys as she got up, grabbed the baby monitor in one hand and the bucket of stain in another. "Jeremy, go get Mommy the big paint brush off the wall behind Daddy's workbench in the garage, please." Meagan spent the next two hours in the back yard slapping stain on the cedar play set. She was surprised to find that once she started working, her energy slowly returned and she found herself enjoying listening to the boys play cars on the patio. When she was finished, the sense of accomplishment filled her. Greg would be so pleased. She was glad to have the chore out of the way.

When Greg came home from work, she took him into the backyard and just listened to the boys tell her husband what a great job she had done on their play set. Greg acknowledged her efforts and said, "I know you hate painting, honey, but I really wanted us to be able to enjoy the weekend without worrying about this, so thanks for doing it." Meagan realized she had demonstrated respect for her husband in front of her kids, modeling for them something very important. She also realized she had shown him love in a very tangible way. That opportunity would have been missed had she stayed on the couch!

Bottom Line: God helps us in our relationships, but only when we listen to His still, soft voice. Choose to listen and your family will benefit!

So What About You?

1) What chore nags at you that you keep putting off?

2) Go through your house. What room needs the most work right now? Perhaps it is your backyard or the garage. Go to that area now and make a "master list" of the tasks you can complete to create order. Put the list in your calendar and do one item per day until they are completed.

3) If your house is in order, ask God for some other area of your life that needs organizing – maybe it's your relationships, health activities, or a work project. What, if anything, are you sensing?

So many times, we get caught up in the lie of being too busy. Often we are just making choices to do too much.

Just because it is a good thing to do, doesn't mean God wants us doing it. Being so busy can make us tired, both emotionally and physically.

Today, your dare includes two items:

1) Take 15 minutes to prayerfully evaluate all the activities in which you are involved. Ask God to reveal to you which are the ones that He has chosen for you to do, and which are ones you should not be doing. Figure out how to un-commit yourself, if possible, and contact those involved. Let them know when your involvement will end.

2) Today and in the following days, start a new habit of asking your husband on a daily basis for one small thing you can do for him, then do it.

Pray that God helps you be wise about what you say, "Yes," to. Remember that it is often stealing a blessing from someone else when we take a job that we are good at, but not called to do.

Pray as well for the opportunity to bless your husband by doing simple things for him on a daily basis.

Dear God,

Dare 14
Treat Him Like A Man

☐ **Dare 14: Treat Him Like A Man**

Proverbs 31:12
She brings him good, not harm, all the days of her life.

As you go through *The Respect Dare*, you are probably starting to be more aware of how other couples communicate with each other. Watch a husband's reactions when you see disrespectful communication from his wife. Many times, there is a subtle gritting of teeth.

A Daughters Story...

Standing and waiting on Bob and Joan's front porch, Karen realized they apparently didn't hear the doorbell ring. Nor were they aware Joan's voice was coming over the intercom at the front door as they set up the crib. "That's not right, it pops up here first! No, not like that, like this! No, push that side in first, and then pull it up. Bob, you're still not doing it right."

The wife's comments nipped at Karen's ears as she waited and grew more uncomfortable. She rang the doorbell again. "Go get the door and I'll just do this myself!" she bossed at her husband, Bob.

The man, clearly irritated, answered the door. "Bob, it's good to see you!" Karen smiled. "I just wanted to drop dinner off for you and your wife. How's the new baby?" He smiled and launched into a story about life with a newborn and she could see him relaxing.

About five minutes later, his wife came to the door, "Oh, thank you for bringing dinner!" she said. "Bob, you better get that in the refrigerator. The lettuce will wilt if it gets warm." His brow furrowed, his lips pursed a bit, he nodded at Karen and left. She felt sorry for the guy. Here's a man who daily runs a crew of 30 guys on a construction job, and his wife talks to him like he's a five year old.

In the car on her way home, Karen grimaced as she remembered someone asking her at a social gathering about ten years before, "How many children do you have?" "Three, if you count my husband," Karen had replied. Since then, she had heard similar responses from many women over the years. She was sure that back then, her behavior matched her attitude. How could it be that she could think about her own husband as if he were a child? She felt a slight twang of guilt and remorse for her actions. She also realized that Joan was on the same path in her marriage.

Karen was thankful she had learned that her behavior was rooted in disrespect and that it was not honoring to her or her husband. Maybe she could recommend a *Daughters of Sarah* class to Joan in the future.

Bottom Line: Think about and treat your husband as the man God created him to be. If you do, your husband will feel more respected by you and your marriage will improve.

So What About You?

1) Ask your husband if he feels like he has ever been treated like a child by you. Ask him how this has made

him feel, and apologize if necessary. How has treating him like this been harmful to your marriage and to him?

2) Can you remember your mother, sisters, or friends talking about their husbands as though these men were inferior? How has this impacted families?

3) Make a list of eight things that wives (in general) can do to make their husbands feel like men:

    a. _____

    b. _____

    c. _____

    d. _____

    e. _____

    f. _____

    g. _____

    h. _____

4) Pick two that you feel would benefit your husband's esteem the most and circle them.

5) Either schedule these activities or do them today, without expectations. What <u>specifically</u> are you going to do and when? Write it here:

Often we give to others with the expectation that our gift will be rewarded. Recognize that this type of "giving" is not a true "gift" if it is actually "sold" for praise or appreciation. Christ gave the gift of His life for ours by dying on the cross. Before that, He repeatedly gave healing, teaching, and food to those in need without expectation of payment or even appreciation. His behavior is the perfect example of love. It is God's love for us, brought to life in the man of Christ Jesus. From this day forward, when you experience resentment or disappointment due to your husband's reaction (or lack of reaction), consider those feelings cues of expectations for you. Choose in those moments to change your attitude, loving without expectation, as God did through Jesus Christ.

Pray for God's help in doing this.

Dear God,

Dare 15
Where's Your Treasure?

☐ **Dare 15: Where's Your Treasure?**

Hebrews 13:5
Keep your lives free from the love of money and be content with what you have, because God has said, "Never will I leave you; never will I forsake you."

Many times it takes a crisis for us to appreciate what's really valuable in life. As we take a peek into the lives of this couple right after they've been robbed, we have the opportunity to focus on what really matters.

A Daughters Story...

Justine and Larry walked back into the living room and sat down. After showing the police officer to the door, she and her husband sat for a few moments on the couch in silence. "What was the money for?" she asked him.

"I was saving it to surprise you on our anniversary. It was for new furniture for this room. Figured the $8,000 would have covered it," he replied.

"How long had you been saving it?" she inquired.

"About four years. Worst thing is that the only person who knew that money was there was Darrin, but I suppose a desk drawer is a common place where thieves look."

Justine felt her pulse quicken and her temper flare. Darrin, Larry's 21-year-old son from a prior marriage, had been in and out of jail over the last two years. Two weeks ago, he had shown up at the house drunk, demanding money. "What are you going to do?" Justine asked.

"You know, I told the police about him, and whatever happens, happens," he began. "I love him, but I can't protect him from his choices. I'm not even certain he did it. What matters most is that we were gone. I don't know what I would have done if something had happened to you or the kids. Yeah, I'm upset about the money, upset about Darrin, but you matter most to me." Larry put his arm around her and pulled her close.

Sitting there, with her cheek against his chest, the smell of his aftershave and the warmth of his body comforted her. Three days later at her *Daughters of Sarah* class, she told the group, "I have always loved my husband, but he and I have never been best friends. After the robbery, I understood fully what it is like to have intimacy on a relational level with my husband. I can tell you that we are best friends now. It's because I've learned how to respect him."

A month later, when Justine's class graduated, her husband, though sick with the flu, attended. He wasn't about to let anyone else put the pearl and sterling silver commencement bracelet she had earned on her wrist.

Bottom Line: Marriages who have love and respect know where their true treasures lie – in each other. Contentment with each other trumps the material things in our lives any day!

So What About You?

1) Do you ever find yourself envious of what your friends or family members have? How does that affect you?

2) Do you ever put pressure on your husband to get a raise or promotion so you can afford to spend more money? Why or why not?

3) What do you think about the Biblical concept that the money we have and the things we own aren't really ours but are instead tools to be used to do work for God?

4) Do you trust God enough to provide for your needs, or do you hold tightly to whatever you have? Why or why not?

5) What do you sense God is trying to teach you through today's verse?

Many people do not realize how fortunate they are. In a 2005 study from the World Bank, the average American's standard of living demonstrates greater wealth than most people on the entire globe experience. [2]
One of the main issues for us in our relationship with God and our relationship with our husband is how content we are with our circumstances.

Today's dare has two steps:
1) Do an online search on poverty or visit your local library to read about conditions in which the majority of people in the world live. Spend at least 30 minutes learning what and when they eat, what diseases they face, and what their struggles are.
2) After doing this research, thank your husband for providing for your family, even if you are working as well. Studies demonstrate that regardless of a wife's employment situation, men are driven to be the provider for their families.[3] If your husband does not currently have a job, thank him for whatever he is doing, whether that be helping at home, or looking for work.

Prayerfully thank God for giving you what you have, and always being with you to carry you through to the next step. Include your husband in this prayer of thanksgiving.

Dear God,

Dare 16
Dusty Chandeliers

☐ **Dare 16: Dusty Chandeliers**

Ephesians 4:29
Do not let any unwholesome talk come out of your mouths, but only what is helpful for building others up according to their needs, that it may benefit those who listen.

Sadly, few of us ever even think about having a positive purpose in speaking with someone else. Much of our communication occurs simply because there is a problem to solve or work to be done, as opposed to intentionally taking an opportunity to encourage our spouse.

A Daughters Story...

Kelly rolled over and looked at the clock; it was 9:24 a.m. on Saturday morning. Working long hours and on weekends, she couldn't remember the last time she'd slept that late. She heard some banging and guessed that Travis was making breakfast. She put on her robe and slowly walked to the kitchen, carefully avoiding the ladder standing in the middle of the entryway. "Coffee?" he asked upon seeing her.

"Thanks," she smiled, noticing that he was fully dressed and appeared to have been up for quite some time. Looking around the kitchen, she noticed that he wasn't making breakfast, but rather repairing the faucet in the sink. "What are you doing?" she inquired.

"Well, I thought I'd get this drippy faucet fixed. I already replaced the bulbs in the chandelier in the entry way and figured I should get this faucet repaired before we go to your mother's this afternoon," he replied.

"Wow," she said. After drinking her coffee and getting dressed, she once again walked around the ladder in the entryway. She stopped and looked at the chandelier. They had lived in this house for 10 years, and she didn't think the light had ever been dusted. Looking at it now, she was surprised that her husband would have replaced the several burned out bulbs, but not cleaned it properly, as cobwebs still hung from the fixture. "You're not done with this chandelier, are you?" she asked him, walking back in the kitchen.

"Yes, I am, I just haven't put the ladder away yet. And in a minute, I'll be done with this faucet, too," he replied.

"Why didn't you clean the chandelier? You always leave things about half done," Kelly said, scowling. As soon as the words left her mouth, she wished she could take them back. In front of her, she saw her husband go from being pleased with his work, to frowning at her. "Oh, my! That was really disrespectful of me, wasn't it?" she realized. "I have just belittled all the hard work you've done this morning, while you let me sleep in! I am really sorry. Sometimes I just say stupid things and that was one of them." He seemed to soften a little. "Travis, I really am thankful that you have worked so hard around here today, honey," she began again. "Please forgive me for being insensitive."

Travis shrugged his shoulders, smiled, and said, "No problem. Thanks for noticing. If you want the chandelier dusted, I can do it later, okay?"

Bottom Line: Speak words of encouragement, but if you screw up, apologize quickly! Recognizing what is good in a situation first will always help you relationally, while criticism guarantees you trouble.

Many times, we miss seeing what is done well or right in a circumstance because it is in our nature to focus on the negative.

Today, your dare is very simple. Not easy, but simple. Regardless of what happens, as an experiment to help you understand your nature, only call attention to what is right or good in a situation. Refuse to find fault with anything your coworkers, friends, husband, or children, have done or not done for the duration of the day. Wear a rubber band around your wrist or wear your watch on your opposite arm to remind yourself of this throughout the day.

You will reflect on the day in the questions on the next page, after you have completed this dare. If you find yourself tearing someone down or finding fault with a situation, immediately apologize and go back to finding what is right or good, then speak only about those things.

You will need God's help in accomplishing this, so be certain to ask Him to show you what is right and good before you begin.

So What About You?

1) Were you able to achieve the dare?

2) Why or why not?

3) What was easy or hard about this dare?

4) Was the dare easier with people who are "close" to you or "acquaintances?" Why?

5) Did you ever find yourself struggling with pride instead of apologizing? Why is it easy to apologize or hard for you to do so.

6) What do you feel God is teaching you through this verse today?

> Pray for God's help in becoming an encouraging person in your marriage and your life on a daily basis.

Dear God,

Dare 17
Sweet Words

☐ **Dare 17: Sweet Words**

Proverbs 16:24
Pleasant words are a honeycomb, sweet to the soul and healing to the bones.

Sometimes we just need to ask for positive feedback. Hearing accolades about ourselves should never be our motive for changing, but when we feel down, our spouse can often lift us up in ways no other individual on the planet is capable of doing. Give him the chance.

A Daughters Story...

Nick brought the dishes he cleared from the table into the kitchen and stood by his wife, who was at the sink staring out the window. "You're going to be late," he said.

"I don't think I'm going to go," Emily replied.

"Why not?" he prodded.

"I'm just not as far as I thought I'd be by now in the course. I keep thinking I'm going to be different, and yet all I see are my failures," she answered.

"What are you talking about?" Nick was incredulous. "I have seen so many changes in you!" he said.

"Really? Like what? I'm supposed to talk about how I've done with my commitment tonight and I feel like I haven't made any progress at all! What changes are you talking about?" Emily doubted he would have much to say now.

"Oh, Em, you're just different. You're more confident. You make decisions better. You don't worry as much. There's a sense of peace about you that hasn't been there before. And you're nicer to me. You notice every single day when I come home from work, and you seem really interested in me as a person again. It's like you're that girl I fell in love with 14 years ago. I really like it that you say nice things to me once in a while now. I enjoy hearing that I'm doing a good job, and I like it that you thank me for going to work in the morning, as corny as that may be." He stopped and looked at her. "You need to leave now or you're going to be late. I'll get the dishes."

She stared at him, now her turn to be incredulous. She had no idea that in five short weeks, she had turned the cold, black lump of resentment in her heart into what she truly did feel now, which was peace. He was right. She <u>was</u> different. Her commitment had been to trust God with all her might, and as a result, she had stopped worrying and had new peace in her life. Grabbing her purse and coat, she headed out the door to tell the class about her conversation with Nick. She also made a mental note to let him know more often how much she values all he does and the man he's become. She felt great and wanted him to also feel that same way.

Bottom Line: If you want to find out how you are doing, check in with your husband. His perspective will not only enlighten you, but remind you of what God is doing in your life.

So What About You?

1. Think of 5 things your husband does, consistently, every single week and write them here (takes out the garbage, goes to work, etc.)

   a. _____
   b. _____
   c. _____
   d. _____
   e. _____

2. Now write down a strength that each of those activities represent, i.e.: if he goes to work every day, he's a provider; if he takes out the garbage, he demonstrates responsibility; etc.)

   a. _____
   b. _____
   c. _____
   d. _____
   e. _____

3. Now write down what each of those strengths means to you, why it's important, why you appreciate it. For example: if you had "takes out garbage," for 1 and "is responsible" for 2, for 3a you might write, "let's me catch an extra 30 minutes of sleep," or, "makes me feel like he cares about the house." or, Or whatever! Write one for each:

   a. _____
   b. _____
   c. _____
   d. _____
   e. _____

4.   Now, turn each one of those into a single note (for a total of 5 notes) and hide them where he will find them over the course of a week. Put them on the steering wheel of his car, in his laptop or briefcase, in his underwear drawer; mail one to him at work, etc.

Have no expectation that your husband will notice or say even a single word about receiving these notes. You are doing this to build him up and encourage him. This is an opportunity to give him a gift in the purest sense without a single expectation.

Thank God for what He has already done in your spiritual life (be specific). Pray that He gives you His level of love to heap upon your man.

Dear God,

Dare 18
Fighting Fair

☐ **Dare 18: Fighting Fair**

Proverbs 15:1
A gentle answer turns away wrath, but a harsh word stirs up anger.

A Daughters Story...

Dan and Kris waited for their food to arrive as they talked about the movie. "I don't think they did a good job with the woman," Kris said.

"It was all about how the man needed to change, and the wife was the one having the affair." Dan agreed.

"Do you feel respected by me?" asked Kris, referring to one of the man's major complaints about his wife in the film.

"Most of the time, although you aren't so great at receiving feedback – sometimes you get defensive," he replied.

A pause followed. Kris knew he was going to ask her if she felt loved. Should she tell him the truth? "Do you feel loved by me?" he asked.

"No," she replied. "On an intellectual level, I know that you love me, but no, I don't experience that knowledge on an emotional level." Silence ensued.

"Why not?" he asked.

Kris struggled to answer. She couldn't believe he didn't know the answer. She had complained, nagged, reminded, joked, emailed, coached, begged, cried, and finally given up on hearing anything other than criticism from her husband after trying to please him for 20 years. Instead of responding in anger, however, she gently said, "Dan, I know you love me. You go to work every day to provide for our family. You do things around the house to take care of us. I appreciate that. You've said repeatedly you don't do the 'warm fuzzy' stuff well, and that you can't change. The question you asked me was, do I feel "loved" by you, and I don't. I do know what you think about the tender side of love, and it's just going to make us feel bad to continue this discussion, so let's talk about something else. I'm sorry I've tried to make you into someone you are not all these years."

After staring at her for several seconds, Dan said, "Why did you ask me if I felt respected by you?"

Kris met his eyes and responded, "Part of who I am at the core is someone who always strives to do better. If I'm not getting the respect piece right, I'm not doing what God wants from me, either, and that's not okay."

Dan seemed a little out of sorts over the next several days. Kris did her best to continue to affirm him daily, but clearly his mind was elsewhere. One day the doorbell rang and there stood a florist with 2 dozen red roses. The card attached read, "Each one of these pales in its beauty compared to you. Each represents a strength I see in you daily: perseverance, faithfulness, confidence, leadership, tenderness," and the list went on and on.

Kris taped it to the inside of her coffee and tea cabinet where she would see it each morning and remind herself of her husband's love for her. She was thankful for the frankness of their discussion, but even more thankful that she had spent the last seven years working on respect. She had ceased complaining and expecting her husband to change. She lived her life knowing what she did on a daily basis was pleasing to God. She was also thankful she had responded like a mature woman - honest but gentle. Instead of having an argument, she communicated clearly and her husband responded.

Over the following weeks, she started seeing little changes in Dan. At least once a day he thanked her for making dinner, complimented her on how she looked, or noticed a chore she had completed for him. Kris was able to enjoy these little blessings immensely because she didn't expect them.

Bottom Line: Loving communication is gentle, honest, and without malice or anger. When wives get the respect piece right, and are more discerning about what they say, their husbands hear them more clearly.

So What About You?

1) Think about the last several days and the conversations you have had with people over the phone, in person and via email. If you were to weigh the sheer number of words of each person, or the time each of you spent speaking, where would you fall on the scale compared to the others? Do others account for more than half of the words spoken or do yours?

2) Do people look as though they are continually trying to get a word in edgewise when speaking with you? What typically describes other peoples' nonverbal cues when they are conversing with you?

3) Are you known to be a good listener? If the answer is yes, you probably are. If you've never received that compliment, that should let you know you have some serious work to do!

4) Have you ever repeated back to a person what they said in order to establish empathy or clarity? Pick one example and describe it below:

5) How does today's verse and story connect with you?

Have you ever listened so long to someone that you started tuning out? Women use more words in an average day than men do. Much in the same way that having a birthday cake every day would lessen its specialness once a year, the number of words we speak can cloud the messages that actually are heard by those around us. What is important can often get lost in the sheer volume of communication when we attempt to engage with our spouse. We know from experience and research that if we speak frequently, our husband has a difficult time discerning what is important amidst the abundance of information. Speaking less has an impact because it highlights what is important. Choose from this day forward to speak fewer words and make those count. If you need to vent, do so with God or a trusted friend who will point you back to Him. Pray for God's help in speaking less, so others will know when you speak, it matters and isn't constant "drivel" to be ignored.

Dear God,

Dare 19
17 Frying Pans

☐ **Dare 19: 17 Frying Pans**

1 Corinthians 14:33, 40
For God is not a God of disorder but of peace...But everything should be done in a fitting and orderly way.

The number 17 is not an exaggeration, and it speaks to our nature as Americans to hold tightly to our possessions. There is great freedom in living plainly, simply, and in an organized fashion.

A Daughters Story

Susan wandered in the house from a morning meeting for her part-time job and stared in shock at the disaster in her kitchen. The contents of all the cabinets lined the counters, the table, covered the chairs and even the floor. "What have you done?" she inquired incredulously.

"You and I both know this kitchen is inefficiently set up, Susan. You have too much stuff and I want to make your life easier," her sister replied. Kristi had come to live with them during a separation from her husband. Susan, a communications professional, coached Kristi on her communication with her husband, while Kristi helped Susan get her house organized. "Are you aware that you have 17 frying pans?" Kristi asked.

"Well, I knew I had a lot, but didn't realize we had that many! Jeff has different ones for different things, and they're all different sizes. There's a few in there for doing eggs and I know there's one for crepes. Then there's some that are cast iron in different sizes, and a few that are non-stick and one that's aluminum. Um, we both had a bunch when we got married, and then we purchased a few more…" Susan replied somewhat sheepishly.

"Have you heard of Goodwill?" Kristi asked. "Go get Jeff and find out which of these you actually use," she ordered. Susan did so, and after much discussion, they had nine pans in a box for Goodwill. She and Kristi spent the rest of the day putting the kitchen back together, using efficiency concepts. Instead of her spatulas being in a drawer all the way across the room from the stove, they ended up in a pretty pitcher next to the stove, so she didn't even have to take a step to grab them. The spices were also placed next to the stove, where they could be accessed easily. They put the dishes where the children could access them more easily to set the table, and moved the paper products to a seldom-accessed cabinet for storage purposes. The box for Goodwill continued to fill until they had to make another one. Five Goodwill boxes later, the kitchen was finished. The two women stood back and admired the job. Jeff came in and received the grand tour. After thanking the women for their work, he added, "I've always thought this could be more orderly – it's set up intuitively now and should work better."

Bottom Line: Run your home in an orderly way, keeping only what you truly need, and you will have less clutter and more peace!

So What About You?

1) Often people either have a place for everything and everything in its place, or piles of items all over the entire home. Do you fall in either category or somewhere in between?

2) Clutter and disorganization are often life-stage issues, so give yourself some grace if you are suffering from a physical impairment or have little kids in the home. Keeping that in mind, what, if anything, needs to be organized in your home? Make a list of the rooms or areas:

3) What would change in your life if you had more order to your home?

4) What about your work? If you have a cubicle or office, what needs to be organized in that space? Make a list:

5) What would change for you at work if you were more organized?

Many of us are planning to fail by failing to plan. Inaction is also a decision. Today's challenge is to spend 17 minutes right now prioritizing your lists from today's questions. Specify tasks for each room. Use a timer to create a sense of urgency and keep the exercise from turning into an hour.

Print out your lists with the tasks and tape them to your refrigerator. Each day, using a timer, spend just 20 minutes working on the top priority task until it is completed. Check it off when you are done and move to the second priority task and so on, until your list is complete.

Before starting any of this, however, pray that God will help you become more organized and orderly in the way you live your life.

Dear God,

Dare 20
Blow Dryer Briefs

☐ **Dare 20: Blow Dryer Briefs**

Philippians 2:3-4
Do nothing from selfishness or empty conceit, but with humility of mind regard one another as more important than yourselves; do not merely look out for your own personal interests, but also for the interests of others.

We marveled at this woman's innovative solution to a problem. Instead of being grumpy or getting stressed out, she chose a cheerful attitude and had fun solving a problem. Life is always more fun and interesting when we choose a good attitude!

A Daughters Story...

Dana ran downstairs, knowing her husband would be getting dressed in about 25 minutes. Working late last night, she had turned the washer on with a full load of whites, but forgotten to change it over to the dryer before collapsing into bed. She quickly threw a single pair of her husband's briefs into the dryer and started it, then went into the kitchen to brew the coffee. Her husband's alarm went off and she estimated she had about 20 more minutes before he would need his underwear. She took coffee for both of them up to their room and proceeded to get dressed for work herself. The minutes ticked by as Jim took his shower and wrapped in a towel, began to shave. She put on her make up and did her hair, skipping her opportunity to shower. Hearing the dryer buzzer, she raced downstairs to find the briefs still a bit damp. Up the stairs she went again, thinking she might be able to pull this off while he was shaving.

"What are you doing with my underwear?" he asked, staring curiously at her as she plugged the blow dryer into the outlet.

"Creative solution," she smiled, blow-drying his briefs. "I'll have them ready for you in just a few minutes."

"Wow, um, thanks!" Jim replied.

Five minutes later, the underwear was almost completely dry. "The band is still a teeny bit damp, but the rest is dry," she said as she held them out to him.

"Great – I don't think you've ever blow dried my underwear before," Jim said, "it's a little weird, but I really appreciate you doing that for me."

Dana giggled at the silliness of the whole thing and soon found herself in Jim's arms, giving him a hug and a kiss. She smiled to herself, vowing to plan a little better to avoid running into the same underwear crisis in the future.

Bottom Line: Love sacrificially and creatively, and you will speak volumes to your husband!

So What About You?

1) People typically experience love the way they are most comfortable receiving it. If you think about the way your husband most frequently demonstrates his affection for you, that is probably the way he most easily receives love from you. In what way do you think he most readily receives love from you? Is it an act of service, receiving a gift, affirming words, or something else?

2) What 3 things can you do this week to demonstrate love to your husband in a way he can "hear" it? Make a list:

      a. _____
      b. _____
      c. _____

3) Set a time to accomplish each of those:

      a. _____
      b. _____
      c. _____

4) How will you deal with your expectations if he does not notice what you have done?

Your husband may be insensitive.

You may have come all this way and not even received a single "Thank you," or had him notice anything that you've done. Recognize right now that your selflessness has not gone unseen nor are you alone in this experience.

Over 2000 years ago, God sent his very own son to earth to teach, to heal, and to die, all for people who were insensitive, ungrateful, and oblivious to who He was, and turned their backs on Him.

You are not alone if you love your man sacrificially and he is unaware.

Perhaps God allows this to occur so we can get a picture of what God did for us.

Perhaps He allows this to grow persevering love within us. Perhaps there are other reasons.

Your challenge today has two parts.

1) Reflect on this concept of sacrificial love, discussing it prayerfully in your spirit with God, writing down any enlightening thoughts He brings to you.
2) Begin taking action toward the three demonstrations of love from the earlier questions.

Pray for God's help loving others the way that Jesus loves us.

Dear God,

Dare 21
R-E-S-P-E-C-T

☐ **Dare 21: R-E-S-P-E-C-T**

Ephesians 5:33b
And the wife must respect her husband.

A Daughters Story...

Sharon was at a small gathering of women the other night, when the hostess's husband popped his head in to say, "Hello," and ask if there was anything they needed. They thanked him for his inquiry, a little conversation developed, and he shared that he cooked dinner that night. "It turned out pretty good, I thought," he reported. "I had a salad, there was an entrée and pasta, and even a small dessert!"

His wife rolled her eyes and began, "I don't want you all thinking he's like this all the time," she joked. "He's really not that helpful and on any given night, I'm the one doing most of the work," she continued. Her husband had a very subtle reaction – his body stiffened, he smiled through clenched teeth, and his brow furrowed just a bit. He left shortly after that comment.

While the other women were laughing at what his wife probably considered some good-natured teasing, apparently he didn't agree. Sharon noticed a few of the gals looking at each other with a "Do you believe she just said that?" wide-eyed look on their faces.

When she arrived home, she found her husband, Todd, reading in bed. She related to him what happened and

121

asked him what he thought about it. "She embarrassed him in front of others," he replied. "And he has to stand there and take it like a man, otherwise he's a wimp. If this were reversed, if he had said all that about her in front of his friends, she'd be having a fit. Men get made fun of by women all the time and we're expected to just take it. It bugs us though. He probably won't be too motivated to make dinner for her again."

"Wow. I had no idea." Sharon inquired.

"His wife could have taken the opportunity to say something nice about him in front of her friends and make him feel like a million dollars, or she could have done nothing, and that still would have been positive because you gals were impressed already. What she did was take him down a few notches in public. That's really negative. Why should he serve his wife if all she's going to do is degrade him for his efforts?" Todd replied.

Bottom Line: Respect your husband and he will have more of a servant's heart toward you and your family.

So What About You?

1) When is the last time you publicly praised your husband?

2) Ask your husband if he can remember a time when you publicly praised him and how it made him feel. Do not respond to the answer he gives. Just gather information, even if he says something negative to you. Be aware, this might be a challenge for you in that your natural tendency may be to defend yourself. What did he say?

3) What did you learn by asking that question?

4) When is the last time you publicly criticized your husband?

5) Ask him if he can remember a time when you publicly criticized him and how it made him feel. Just listen to his response without justifying your actions – you are only gathering information. What did he say?

6) What did you learn by asking that question?

Today your dare is very simple. Plan to compliment your husband by writing "CH" (Compliment Husband) on your calendar once or twice a week when you know you will be with other people, even if it is just your family. If you will be around other people today, do this exercise before you go to bed. Keep it short and simple. "Dave, I really appreciate your caring attitude towards me this week when I've been sick. I noticed you have been coming home a little early to help with dinner and the kids. That has really helped me get through the day." Tell him a strength he has (e.g., a caring attitude) and support it with why that matters to you.

Pray that God enables you to see many different opportunities to praise your husband in front of others once or twice a week, and thank him for the

Dear God,

Dare 22
18 Shirts

□ Dare 22: 18 Shirts

Colossians 3:23-34
Whatever you do, do your work heartily, as for the Lord, rather than for men, knowing that from the Lord you will receive the reward of the inheritance. It is Christ whom you serve.

People will frequently disappoint us because they are imperfect humans. So are we. When we forget about the human nature of those around us, we are setting them up to let us down.

A Daughters Story...

The shirts hanging off the ironing board continued to multiply until Nancy's husband asked if she might have time to iron one of them that week. "I haven't seen my favorite white shirt in about two months," he said.

Nancy didn't reply. She was furious with Michael and ironing those shirts ranked last on her To Do list. Since she was only working part time, she knew that theoretically she should be able to complete more of the housework. The reality was, however, that she was exhausted. The new baby, the kindergartener, and their three-year-old wore her out during the hours she spent with them, not to mention all the additional responsibilities that fell on her shoulders while her husband traveled two weeks a month.

After she drove her son to kindergarten and played with the three year old for half an hour in between nursing their

125

baby girl, she remembered the shirts. "I should just take these into the dry cleaner and have them pressed there," she thought. "Michael hates their starching, though, and they seem to keep shrinking the shirts, so I guess I'm stuck with this. I hate ironing!" She counted them. Eighteen shirts awaited her attention. The baby was down for her morning nap and their three year old was occupied with Play-Doh, so she had some time. She brought out the ironing board into the kitchen where she could see the children and began.

As Nancy undid the buttons on Michael's burgundy oxford, she smiled. He had worn this a few days ago. It was a good color on him and she remembered when she first bought it for him. It was a time several years ago when they had gone shopping before a dinner date one rainy Saturday evening. She smiled as she realized he still made it a priority to date her, even ten years into their marriage.

Hanging up that shirt and picking up the next, she realized this shirt needed to be given to Goodwill. She couldn't believe he had worn it to work! The edges were fraying, the color was a bit faded and it just looked old. Certainly not something a corporate professional should be wearing! She felt a twinge of guilt at taking so long to get the shirts done, and started to sense God revealing to her how hard her husband worked, how much he missed them when he traveled, how much he really valued them all.

In the 60 minutes or so it took to iron the eighteen shirts, she sensed the gentle teachings of God illuminating the truth for her. Occasionally a tear would fall onto one of the shirts, only to be steamed out by the hot iron. Finally, they were done and she hung them all in his closet. She didn't care if Michael even noticed that the shirts were done. This job, begun in resentment, had evolved into a privilege she completed for God.

Nancy laughed as she discovered she had actually benefited and grown from the encounter with God while ironing. Realization hit that much of the work she had been doing around the house always had an expectation of appreciation attached to it. She had forgotten that she was a key player in the partnership God created with her and her husband for their family. Whether Michael noticed anything she did, she knew today that she was precious and important to God. He had shown her Michael's motivations for work – to provide for his family because he deeply loved them. She realized she had been selfish and in prayer, thanked God for His gentle teaching and asked for His help in taking care of her family, particularly Michael. Peace and joy replaced the resentment and anger.

Bottom Line: Do all of your work for God, and it will not matter what the humans in your life think of your efforts.

So What About You?

1) Many professional women struggle with resentment due to household responsibilities. Studies show that even though both partners work, the women still feel responsible for household chores. How are you doing in handling all of your responsibilities? How are you doing with the resentment issue?

2) Have you ever had an experience like Nancy did? Describe:

3) What do you sense God teaching you through today's dare?

4) For whom do you work? Are you constantly expecting human recognition or are you so close to God that you sense His pleasure in what you do? Explain.

Women who work (or have worked) outside the home face different challenges in their marriages. The expectation of reward, born out of the receipt of a paycheck and workplace recognition, can transfer to the home life, creating similar expectations which go unfulfilled. Some women who have never worked outside the home also feel this way.

Today, pray, asking God to reveal to you where your motivations originate and what your expectations are. Ask Him for help in doing your work heartily and only for Him.

Pray that He would remove your desire for human praise and replace it with a deeper connection with Him, such that you sense His pleasure with you, even in the mundane daily aspect of life.

Dear God,

Dare 23
Knight Time

☐ **Dare 23: Knight Time**

1 Peter 3:4
Let it be the hidden person of the heart, with the imperishable quality of a gentle and quiet spirit which is precious in the sight of God.

Something most women do not realize is that regardless of whether they work or not, their husbands are wired to provide for them. In a recent survey, men were asked if given a circumstance where their wives earned enough to support their family's lifestyle, if they would still have a need (the actual word was "compulsion") to provide for their families. Of the 1000 men, 78% responded "Yes." Another shocking revelation from the survey showed that the majority of men work long hours or travel out of love for their wives. They do not enjoy being away from their families, but rather see this as an act of sacrificial giving for their loved ones.

A Daughters Story...

Kim silently looked at the building as her husband parked in front of the entrance. On Monday morning, the financial institution would be alive with people busily settling themselves into their new workspace like hundreds of nesting penguins on a rocky shore. She smiled, thinking that in two days, all of her husband's employees would be carrying and setting down their boxes of supplies, re-creating their own work spaces. For now, however, the desolate parking lot reflected none of the activity to come, but rather made their one car appear lonely on the dark night.

Kim and Mitch walked to the front doors, he punched his code and they entered the building. "Come on, I'll give you the grand tour," he said to her. Walking through the lobby, meeting rooms, large conference center and customer service cubicles, Mitch talked excitedly, letting her know his plans for the organization, and Kim eagerly listened to him. "And this is where my office will be," Mitch explained, opening the door to a fairly good-sized room on the top floor. The dark cherry desk and bookcases looked lovely with the green walls. She could see the park across the street through the window, and noticed a familiar object on the sill. She walked across the room and picked the porcelain knight up, turning it gently in her hands. "I wanted to see it every time I walked into this office," Mitch said.

"I'm so proud of you," Kim began. "I can't believe all you've accomplished in the last five years!" When Mitch had taken over the organization several years back, it had been close to bankruptcy, and now, even in a challenging economy, profits had skyrocketed and they had built a new home office. Kim remembered the day she had given Mitch the knight. He had been engulfed in a particularly difficult two month period, restructuring the organization to make it more efficient. "Don't forget Whose army you march in, and thank you for being my knight in shining armor on a daily basis." she had told him as she handed him the box with the knight in it.

That evening, as she secretly watched, he placed the knight all around the main floor of their home. After watching him move it about six times, she had finally asked, "Mitch, what are you doing?"

"I want to see it both when I leave for work and when I get home. It reminds me of what you really think of me, and that my work is for the Lord," he replied.

Now, looking at the knight standing on the window sill of Mitch's company's new building, she was pleased to see the statue still spurred her husband on to do the next thing. "Congratulations honey," she said warmly to him. "I'm so proud of you!"

Bottom Line: Find ways to encourage your husband and build him up instead of tearing him down and you will help him accomplish his dreams.

So What About You?

1) When have you taken the opportunity to celebrate a success of your husband's?

2) What tangible evidence of your respect and admiration could you present to your husband?

3) What would be your goal in doing that? How would you deal with his potential lack of favorable or enthusiastic response?

Today, your dare is three-fold. Challenge yourself to complete these tasks in order, by the end of the day:

1. Write yourself a brief letter, reminding yourself to pay attention only to pleasing God instead of seeking earthly reward and recognition from other humans. Write as though you were speaking to a younger, newly married woman about her relationship with God being more important than her relationship with her husband.

2. Seek an opportunity to give a gift to your husband – search online for a knight, sword, medal, etc., that you could give to him that would remind him of his manhood and of your admiration for him. If unable to afford something, take a small piece of paper that fits in his wallet and write him a short note explaining to him why you view him as your knight in shining armor and what he (or his position) means to your family.

3. Ask God to help you remember to live your life for the Audience of One on a daily basis.

Dear God,

Dare 24
Quiet Time

☐ **Dare 24:** Quiet Time

1 Peter 3:1B-2

They may be won without a word by the behavior of their wives, as they observe your chaste and respectful behavior.

Many people crave an intimate relationship with God but simply don't know how to go about it. Asking Him for help in that area is a good place to start. Being open to experiencing God is another.

A Daughters Story...

Turning off the light and placing her book on the nightstand, Rebecca prayed before going to sleep, "Lord, I want to spend time with you first thing tomorrow morning. Please help me get up!" She closed her eyes, and imagined herself, child-sized and cradled in the lap of God Himself. She envisioned the Creator of the Universe gently stroking her hair until she fell asleep...

Hours later, Rebecca awakens in the dark. She rolls over to look at the alarm clock and discovers that it is 5:43am. Two minutes remain before her alarm sounds. Tempted to close her eyes and then hit the snooze a few times, she sits up in bed and shuts the alarm completely off for the day. Last night she prayed that God would awaken her easily this morning so she could spend time with Him, and of course, He was faithful. The least she could do was her little part and actually get out of bed. She looked over at her husband and saw Jack still sleeping. Without a noise, she sneaks out of the bedroom and down the stairs.

After brewing the coffee and pouring herself a cup, she sat down in her favorite chair and read today's date in J. Oswald Chambers', *My Utmost for His Highest*. Since it was the 21st day of the month, she then read that chapter of Proverbs, that great book of wisdom, as was her habit. Wanting to understand the man Jesus, who was also God, she turned to the story where Jesus walks on water and encourages Peter to do the same. She then moved to one of her favorite parts of her daily time with God; that of imagining herself inside the story, as if she was actually there with Christ – a prayer method practiced and written of by St. Ignatius.

She closes her eyes, and imagines herself in the boat with the other disciples, and sees Jesus walking towards her across the lake. Mist surrounds Him, and she can see his bare feet on the surface of the water as if it were solid glass covered by half an inch of liquid. "Come," He says to her, and she grabs the rough wooden side of the boat and takes a step confidently onto the wet surface. She doesn't sink. Lost in the imagery, her heart begins to race. Rebecca looks up and her eyes lock with what she perceives as incredible power emanating from the depths of the bright blue pools of His eyes. Her knees shake and she looks away, intimidated. She sees waves forming in the water around her. The wind begins to blow. Spray from the water stings her skin like needles. Her hair catches in her mouth as she glimpses what appear to be hideous faces on the cusps of the waves. The snarling mouths gape open and razor-sharp teeth reach for her shins and ankles. Horrified, she looks up at Jesus, and realizing she is starting to sink, thrusts her hands out toward Him. "Lord, save me!" she cries. He grasps her firmly, and pulls her to her feet. "You of little faith," He says to her, "why did you doubt?"

Rebecca sits quietly and waits to sense a leading from God. "Teach me," she prays and waits. Moments pass and just as she has nearly decided that she probably needs to ponder what she's read and experienced for the day, she has a sense of knowing she needs to "just get out of the boat." She asks, "Where?" and images of ideas for a children's program at her church start to flood her mind. "Thank You, Father," she whispers...

She heard Jack's footsteps in the hall stop and she knew he was watching her pray. After thanking God for their time together this morning, and pleased she has been a witness to her husband in such a small and simple way, she raises her head, opens her eyes, and greets her husband. She can't wait to talk to him about what she thinks she's being led to do. She knew also, that if God confirmed it through Jack and perhaps a few other circumstances, she would be on the right track.

Bottom Line: Cultivate your own relationship with God and He will influence others through you. Your steps in life will also be more certain as you are listening to Him.

So What About You?

1) What spoke to you about the Daughters story today?

2) Read Matthew 14:22-33.

3) Imagine yourself in Peter's place, like Rebecca did, and wait at the end of the experience.

4) What, if anything, happened? Did you hold back, or were you freely transparent with Him? Did you feel silly, waiting for something to happen? Did you allow yourself to be vulnerable and authentic?

5) Why do you think it went the way it did?

Do not feel bad if your experience was less than you had hoped. Perhaps at the very least, you realize how comfortable you are being vulnerable with God.

Today your dare is very simple, but perhaps not easy. Take a quantum leap outside your comfort zone and ask God to create in you a soul which longs to experience His presence. Pray He awakens you in the morning to spend time with Him. Ask God to help you carve out moments to be with Him.

Dear God,

Dare 25
Not Always What They Seem

☐ **Dare 25: Not Always What They Seem**

1 Peter 3:8, 9
To sum up, all of you be harmonious, sympathetic, brotherly, kind-hearted, and humble in spirit, not returning evil for evil or insult for insult, but giving a blessing instead; for you were called for the very purpose that you might inherit a blessing.

Many of us get too much exercise by jumping to conclusions. We all need to do a better job of extending grace instead of judgment, and we can often be a positive influence to others as a result.

A Daughters Story...

Completing the work at her computer, Bonnie's fingers sped across the keyboard. She tried to stay focused on the report, however, the voices of the two women next to her cube continued to distract her. "Shannon showed up late again today, even though I'm pretty sure the boss talked to her just yesterday about being late so much!" hissed Nicole.

"Yeah, I noticed," Dana responded. "I'm getting tired of answering the phones for her until she decides to grace us with her presence. I can't believe she hasn't been fired yet!"

Bonnie's fingers froze. Aware of Shannon's recent separation from her husband, she knew her coworker was juggling trying to get two kids to different schools and one to preschool, all before coming in to work in the morning. Never mind all the additional housework and being the only parent shouldering all the responsibilities. She also knew Dave, their supervisor, had given Shannon a bit of a break yesterday and moved her start time from 8:00 to 8:45 a.m.

The two women rounded the corner, ducking their heads into Bonnie's cubicle. "Hey Bonnie, aren't you getting tired of picking up the slack for Shannon? Haven't you had enough of this? We're going to go complain to Dave and were wondering if you wanted to come with us," announced Dana.

"Oh, hi Dana! Hey, how's your son doing? Did the appointment go okay yesterday?" Bonnie inquired, dodging the question.

"Thanks for asking," Dana began, "We still don't know what's causing his illness and are actually thinking of trying that in-hospital procedure." Dana's son frequently suffered from intense headaches and the doctors still had yet to find a cause.

"Well keep me posted, okay? I keep praying for him. So what are you gals talking about with Shannon? She's been having a bit of a hard time lately – didn't know if you were aware of that – but actually I think she could use our help," Bonnie stated.

Dana seemed surprised. "Why? What's going on with her?"

"Well, it's similar to what you're going through with your son, Dana," Bonnie responded softly. "The circumstances are a little different, but essentially it's the same in terms of stress level. I think she could use a little grace from all of us these days. If I remember right, Dave adjusted her hours yesterday to try to help her out, too. He'll probably talk with us about it today," Bonnie finished.

Bottom Line: Many times when we are frustrated with someone else's behavior, we don't have all the information. Mature communicators ask questions and extend grace before becoming angry and, as a result, are a blessing to others.

So What About You?

1) What would change in your relationship with your husband if you returned a perceived insult with a question and some grace?

2) Think of the last time you and your husband had a disagreement. What occurred?

3) Did you take the time to fully understand his opinion before communicating yours to him? Why or why not?

Your dare today is to repeat back your understanding of what someone is saying to you, before you voice your own opinion. Start your sentence with, "If I hear you correctly, you are saying…" Then listen for the response. In doing this, you will become very aware of how well you understand what is actually being said to you.

Pray, asking God to help you honor Him through helping you listen well, regardless of the circumstances. Do your very best to recall what is said to you and the intent behind the communication.

Dear God,

Dare 26
Going to Camp

☐ **Dare 26: Going to Camp**

1 Corinthians 1:10
I appeal to you, brothers, in the name of our Lord Jesus Christ, that all of you agree with one another so that there may be no divisions among you and that you may be perfectly united in mind and thought.

The concept of submission in the Bible is a topic which can cause negative reactions amongst women who do not understand it. Even wives who know their husband will be held responsible for the outcome of his family by God Himself, sometimes still fight for control of their family.

Regardless of what you believe about the topic of submission, a wife who accepts her husband as the "CEO" of their family can significantly reduce the level of conflict in her home. Consider a corporation that had two CEO's - much conflict would ensue. Families are similar. These women can also have more influence than those who are always struggling to be in control. We need to remember that "submission" is simply a military term, meant to solve disagreements and differences of opinion when compromise cannot be reached.

Conversely, women who do not share their opinions with their husbands start to experience resentment and frustration. Their family often does not benefit from their experience. Submission does not mean silence, or becoming a doormat. Healthy relationships exhibit dialogue which respectfully communicates disagreement and creates a partnership.

A Daughters Story...

Lizzie cringed when she heard Stephen talking to their 11 year old, Adam, about Boy Scout Camp. Significantly concerned about the boy going away to a different state for a full week, she had told Stephen she thought it was the wrong thing to do. "He's going to get homesick. He'll want to come home. He'll be a complete mess. He's too young. There will be a ton of boys there who are so much older than he is. I don't want him to go," she barraged him with her motherly anxieties.

"Time to cut a few apron strings, Mom," Stephen had replied. "I don't disagree that he's going to be homesick. I think a lot of what you say is true. However, he's 11 and he needs to go. It will be fine. His friends from the troop will be there as well, and so will Nat's dad. Columbus was 12 years old when he left home for good, Lizzie. Adam's going to be fine."

Listening to them pack and talk about the things he would do while there did absolutely nothing to calm her fears. She knew she was being a little irrational, but even that realization didn't help her make peace with the concept. She decided all she could really do was pray. "Dear God, I have no idea what's going to happen while Adam's at camp next week, but I know You do, and I trust that you have it covered. I give to You all my concerns and worries about his being away from home for that long of a period, and trust that You will take care of him. Amen."

While Adam was away, she prayed every day, and when he returned she eagerly listened to everything that had happened. She was right in some regards - he had become homesick, and he didn't get much sleep, but one thing he mentioned stopped her in her tracks. "Mom, you know

Gavin? That kid that I've been friends with for a while in the troop? He's been going to church ever since he was little, but I didn't see him really living his faith. He was always the last to pitch in for KP, and we always had to hunt him down to get him to pull his weight. Well, I started a conversation with him about all that and did you know he didn't even believe in Jesus? We talked for a long time and when we were done, he and I prayed together and he's decided to believe and put Christ in charge of his life. He's really sorry about all the things he's done in his life and realizes he needs God and he told Him that. And the next day, he was a little different. He was gathering firewood before anyone else was even thinking about the evening camp fire."

Pleased by her son's behavior and a little unsettled that she had almost been a barrier to his attendance, she grabbed Adam. "Come over here," she said as she pulled him into her arms. "I want you to know how proud I am of you for doing that."

So in spite of the many mosquito bites and poison ivy, Lizzie's son had come home with more than several merit badges. He had also helped his friend in an eternal way. Lizzie felt all the hesitation and reservations wiped away.

Bottom Line: Living in peace often means trusting our husband's judgment and God's sovereignty instead of paying more attention to our fear.

So What About You?

1) Many of us have been faced with circumstances where we need to "tow the line" despite misgivings, e.g. in dealings with customers, managing employees, military service. What negative perceptions about the company ensue if a customer witnesses a supervisor and subordinate disagreement? How does this concept apply to parenting when the parents fail to present a unified front to their kids?

2) Corporations have one CEO. Countries have one president, states have one governor and towns have one mayor. Tribes have one chief. Even in nature, when two pack animals try to be in charge, there's conflict, often resulting in a fight to the death. Natural order of animals and social structures is such that they function best with one individual being in charge. When two try to have the same authority, conflicts erupt. In the Bible in 1 Corinthians 11:3 and in the creation story in Genesis, we learn that God created man to be in charge of his family. A result of Adam and Eve's sin was that Eve would desire to control her husband. Like the pain associated with corporate takeovers and the destruction in one country taking over another, conflict and pain ensue when we try to be in charge of the family. Do you struggle with trying

to control your husband? Why or why not? How has this issue manifested itself in your marriage?

3) Some women worry that putting their husband in charge of their family is risky because they do not trust him to do a good job. They may feel that this somehow diminishes them or makes them the equivalent of an irrelevant maid in their own home. God's plan for the organization of family does NOT mean either of those. Still other women don't trust God enough to try His plan. What do you feel is your biggest struggle or fear with putting your husband in charge of your home?

4) Some women fear that their husbands would take advantage of them or treat them badly if they put their man officially in charge of their families. Knowing that God holds husbands to a higher standard because of this leadership position, what is the worst thing that could possibly happen to you if you allowed your husband to have the final say if the two of you disagreed about something and a decision had to be made?

5) What do you sense God could do to take care of that situation if it occurred?

Experience indicates that this issue is critical to alleviating marital stress. Many women who grew up in the feminist movement say they have spent years fighting for respect for themselves, when they could have received the love and intimacy they deeply desired by giving away respect to their husband.

Your dare today is to pray wholeheartedly that God shows you how this concept of allowing your husband to be CEO of your family impacts your marriage. Ask Him to help you be teachable and pray that you learn. Ask Him to give you an understanding of the concept in a way that allows you and your husband to be united in spirit.

Dear God,

Dare 27
3:08am

☐ Dare 27: 3:08am

Galatians 6:2
Carry each other's burdens, and in this way you will fulfill the law of Christ.

Perhaps you have been in dire need at some point in your life and received comfort from a friend or relative. Having someone to walk beside you through a difficult time may have meant very much to you. This is one of the ways God demonstrates His love for us. Whenever you love someone in this way, God loves that person through you.

A Daughters Story...

Edna rolled over and looked at the clock. 3:08am. She turned back and found a dim light emanating from the closet and heard her husband, Charlie, rustling around. She rose out of the bed and wandered over to the walk-in and watched him, oblivious to her presence, dressing for work. "What are you doing? It's three in the morning!" she inquired.

"I can't sleep. I just can't – there's too much to do at work and I need to go in."

"That's crazy – come back to bed," she implored.

Charlie stood in the closet half dressed and looked at her. He ran his hands through his hair and said to her, "What's the point? I won't sleep anyway."

"You don't have to sleep, just let me pray for you," she replied, which then began a several times a week habit they continued for the next several months until his job situation changed. Turning the lamp on low, Edna began to read to him from the Psalms. God's words of comfort and encouragement flowed out of her mouth for over an hour. She heard him snoring and turned off the light. "Dear God," she prayed, "Bless him and keep him. Help him get all that he has to do done. Give him your strength, your perseverance, your wisdom and your guidance. Be with him, Lord, and help him finish this project. Help him be highly regarded among his peers. Make his management look favorably upon him, Lord. Help him find his way through this."

As the months passed, Edna continued to pray for her husband and his job situation. He confided in her about his struggles and she simply listened and did her best to encourage him. Finally, a light appeared at the end of this tunnel. He was able to add staff and after several more weeks, things started getting somewhat back to normal.

Circumstances and a challenging economy found one of Charlie's friends out of work. His wife, Becky, consistently complained about his behavior, whining to both of them about what a "loser" he was.

One night Charlie mentioned this situation to Edna. "I wasn't sure I was going to make it through last year," he begins. "I feel bad for Nick. He probably feels awful right now, especially since Becky isn't supporting and encouraging him at all. Thanks for being there for me when I needed you." Edna felt privileged to have walked through their trial by her husband's side. She had sensed all along that God was using her to turn her husband back to God for strength and comfort. She knew she would never regret the lack of sleep, nor the intimacy she felt being with him and God in the middle of those nights.

Bottom Line: Carry your husband's burdens and walk along side him during troubles, praying your way through it together. Two bound together with God are inseparable.

So What About You?

1) Think of the last time you were in real trouble. Did you go to your husband first or even at all? Why or why not?

2) Have you and your husband had any serious struggles in the years you've been married? List the top three hardest ones:

        a. _____
        b. _____
        c. _____

3) How did you handle these challenges? Did you grow closer together or further apart?

4) How involved was God in the midst of your difficulties? Did you cling to Him together, separately, or not at all?

5) Is there a difficult situation you are dealing with now in which you sense God's direction? How do feel led to respond?

Perhaps you've been blessed with the opportunity to cling to your husband during a really difficult time. Perhaps you've been there for him when he's needed you. Maybe there have been times when you have let him down, too. Ask God to show you those right now.

Your challenge today is to do one or both of two activities with your husband:

1) Make a list of all the "wrongs" your husband has committed against you. Make another list of the "wrongs" you've committed against Him. Take his list and burn it, making an active choice to forgive him. Ask your husband if you can speak to him for a few moments. Show him the list of your wrongs and apologize for the times you've let him down or not stood by him when he's needed you. Let him know you regret losing the opportunity to love him well during that time, and that you are sorry for letting him down. Ask for forgiveness.

2) Tell your husband that you want to go on the record as desiring to stand by him always. Tell him you would like to do whatever it takes to become the person he trust the most and considers his most valued confidante. Tell him you consider it a privilege to pray for him and let him know you will be asking him for prayer requests on a daily basis.

In prayer, ask God to help you achieve these things.

Dear God,

Dare 28
Spice of Married Life

☐ **Dare 28: Spice of Married Life**

1 Corinthians 7:4, 5
The wife does not have authority over her own body, but the husband does. And likewise the husband does not have authority over his own body, but the wife does. Do not deprive one another except with consent for a time, that you may give yourselves to fasting and prayer; and come together again so that Satan does not tempt you because of your lack of self-control.

Sexual intimacy was created by God for a number of reasons. Those reasons include our enjoyment and creating a unique closeness that cannot be experienced in any other way. Intimacy can be, however, a challenging area for many wives. God's plan for our physical relationship with our spouse can be something that is tremendously comforting and deepens our connection with each other.

A Daughters Story...

Lydia pulled the lace panties out of the drawer in the closet and slipped on the matching bra. Glancing at herself in the mirror, she thought, "This ought to get Phil's attention!" She waltzed into the bedroom and climbed into bed next to him, pulled up the covers and waited. He was lying next to her, reading his American history novel. Surely he would notice that she was scantily clad. She waited for the question about why she had come to bed when he did, instead of cleaning up the kitchen or doing another load of laundry. She waited and waited, and finally, hearing him snoring, turned off the light and tried to go to sleep herself.

The next night was nearly an exact repeat of this. "What am I doing wrong?" she wondered to herself. "I'll try again," she thought. This evening, instead of just laying there, waiting for him to notice, she sat up on her elbow, dragged her finger down his sleeve and asked him, "Want to play?"

Immediately Phil stopped reading his novel and looked at her. His eyes wandered from hers down to what he could see of her bra straps and what was showing above the covers on their bed. "What's gotten into you?" he asked, suspiciously.

She just smiled at him, leaned over and when her lips were nearly touching his, softly said, "Why don't you find out?"

Soon after that night, Lydia made a commitment to herself and God that she would do whatever it took to get the spice back into their sex life. Twenty-three years was a long time to be physically intimate with the same man. She started doing research at the library about sex and discovered that 50% of women are considered "low drive," meaning that they need a significant amount of foreplay before they will experience arousal. "That sure explains a lot!" she thought, encouraged she wasn't alone. She was even more relieved to learn that only 30% of women have orgasms from intercourse alone. All these years she thought there was something wrong with her. She felt sorry for the 12-15% of women who never experience an orgasm.

Armed with information and her verse, she was enthusiastic about taking things to a new level in the bedroom with Phil. He wasn't quite sure what had happened to his wife, but he certainly enjoyed the benefits!

Bottom Line: Move forward in the physical aspect of your relationship with your husband – both of you will benefit.

So What About You?

1) Have you and your husband discussed your sex life recently? Are you both satisfied with the frequency of your sexual activities?

2) Have you discussed what both of you want from your sex life? Do you know about how frequently your husband wants to engage in lovemaking?

3) What one thing would make a huge difference for your husband in the area of sex?

4) What do you sense God wants you to know about this area?

This can be a difficult and complicated topic for some women. For instance, if you are an abuse survivor or if your husband is addicted to pornography, you will want to seek additional information about how to address the difficulties you face, if you haven't already. But do take action to move forward in this area. Until you get God's help to heal from these tragedies, your sex life with your husband will not be all it can be.

If you are feeling as though you are uninformed about the topic, get information. The reference section in the back of this book is one place you can start. Today, pray that God helps you overcome any obstacles that stand in the way of physical intimacy for you and your spouse. Challenge yourself to initiate, especially if prompted by the Spirit!

Dear God,

Dare 29
30 Year Drought

☐ **Dare 29: 30 Year Drought**

Hebrews 3:13
But encourage one another daily, as long as it is called Today, so that none of you may be hardened by sin's deceitfulness.

According to the American Academy of Matrimonial Lawyers, pornography damages many marriages and some statistics say that it is involved in two out of three divorces in the United States each year. Even pastors are having a difficult time avoiding the lure, with 37% of them reporting it to be a constant struggle. Men comprise 75% of those who report sexual addictions. [4] Dealing with the ramifications of pornography can feel very similar to an affair. Couples need to work on forgiveness, accountability, and continual growth to overcome this issue.

A Daughters Story...

The two women sat over coffee in Nancy's kitchen. After much discussion about their work and children, Nancy inquired of her friend, "Sarah, how are you really doing?"

Sarah, who managed adult ministries at their church, smiled at her friend. "I can't believe what Ron just told me. He says he wants to help me teach these parents about the risks that pornography poses to their children. He prayed for me before I gave the workshop last weekend." Sarah said, tears leaking out the sides of her eyes.

Nancy stared at her for a moment, and then she remembered. Thirty years ago, Sarah had given her husband, Ron, an ultimatum – choose between pornography and her. He had chosen the porn. They had not been intimate physically since then. For him to show up at her workshop and pray with her was nothing less than miraculous. What else would be in store for this couple? Nancy started to laugh.

"What's so funny?" Sarah asked her.

"I was just thinking about the possibilities that might emerge if his heart is changing. You and I might need to go lingerie shopping one of these days, girlfriend!" she replied.

"You've got to be kidding!" Sarah exclaimed.

"Not at all, baby, not at all! If God can create something new in your man, even after all these years, you need to go for it!" Nancy was delighted for her friend. What a devastating thing to go through - 30 years without sex with your husband. God had moved Ron. Nancy vowed to encourage her friend to move forward as well, whatever that meant, perhaps pursuing her husband physically, even after all these years. God could accomplish just about anything and He was the only One who could truly change another person's heart.

"Well, I suppose it's not out of the question. We'll have to see what happens!" Sarah told her.

Bottom Line: God's timing and our timing are often very different. When God makes a change in someone else's life, be receptive to how that change can impact you!

So What About You?

1) What has significantly changed in you since you were a teenager or in your early twenties?

2) Are there things about your husband you are certain will never change? What are they?

3) Based on what you know of God's character and how He wants us to live, how can failing to recognize changes made by people around us negatively impact their continued growth?

4) What response should we have to changes in others?

5) What sometimes prevents you from responding that way?

6) What small changes have you seen your husband make in the last 30 days? In the last ten years?

7) What have you done to acknowledge those changes? If nothing, what WILL you do and when?

Today's dare is simple, and hopefully easy. Prayerfully consider your husband as the man he has become. Ask God to show you what positive characteristics have developed in Him over the last several years and today, in writing, let him know what those characteristics are. Be specific, and support each one with a reason why it is important to you.

Dear God,

Dare 30
Too Much Skin

☐ **Dare 30: Too Much Skin**

Proverbs 11:22
Like a gold ring in a pig's snout is a beautiful woman who shows no discretion.

Men are more visual than women and struggle in ways that most women cannot even imagine. The magazines in a supermarket checkout line can be a temptation minefield for a man trying to keep his eyes off other women and his thoughts only of his own wife. We can do much for the men around us if we will but choose our clothing a little more carefully.

A Daughters Story...

Claire watched as her husband's eyes strayed from full engagement in conversation with her, to repeated glancing to the left, at someone behind her. "Who are you looking at?" she asked him.

Paul immediately stammered a bit and finally replied, "I can't help it, honey, but we need to move. That woman who just came in is about half-dressed and I can't keep from looking at her."

Claire and Paul switched places in the family room of their friends' home, and she saw exactly what he meant. Across the room, and being noticed by nearly everyone at the company party, was Ronnie. She was a new addition to the staff, and made a habit of wearing short skirts and low-cut blouses; but her attire tonight took the cake. The sleeveless little black dress barely covered the essentials

165

and even though it was December, more of her skin was showing than was covered.

"Where's her husband?" Claire asked Paul.

"I don't see him," he responded. "If I were him I wouldn't have come with her either, the way she looks."

This confused Claire, so she asked him, "Why wouldn't you want to strut around with a trophy wife like that on your arm?"

Paul's answer not only surprised her, but warmed her heart. "Fifteen years ago, I might have, but I've changed a lot, Claire. That girl only wants attention and is doing everything she can to get it. Her husband isn't naïve, either. He probably sees her motives and wants no part. I mean, what man wants all his friends thinking about having sex with his wife? It's pretty sad, too, because he's actually a pretty nice guy."

Claire recalled a study that she had recently read in a book that showed 98% of men who see a visually attractive woman are well aware of her presence to the extent that they think about her repeatedly, even if they don't want to do so.[5] "How do you handle working with her every day?" Claire asked him.

Paul replied, "I stay away from her as much as possible and if I need to, I refocus on pictures of you and the kids." Claire felt a little sorry for Ronnie. She was certain her attempts for attention were fulfilled, but she was obviously acting in an emotionally unhealthy way. Claire appreciated the candor with which Paul communicated the truth to her. While she didn't understand by experience her husband's visual struggles, it certainly motivated her to keep herself fit. She wanted to be sure she was the most affirming and positive woman her husband would encounter on any given day. The thought of Ronnie in Paul's office, vying for attention also made her a little angry.

Bottom Line: We need to be respectful of other women's husbands in the way we dress. Make it easy on your husband's friends and coworkers by dressing conservatively and saving the glamour for hubby!

So What About You?

1. How has our culture convinced women that being sex objects is a good, beautiful thing?

2. What's wrong with this?

3. How does it negatively affect our daughters and young women?

4. How does it negatively affect us?

5. What about your own clothing? Do you dress modestly?

6. In general, most men struggle with visual images and sexual thoughts when exposed to cleavage, short skirts, etc. Men will also say that when watching a presentation given by a provocatively dressed woman, they aren't listening to what she's saying, but rather thinking about her body or what it's like to have sex with her. How do you feel about that? Would you rather have men hearing what you have said or have them thinking sexual thoughts about you?

Today your dare is relatively simple.

Prayerfully spend 15 minutes going through your closet. Consider what your clothing is communicating about you and how it represents your husband and family. Are there things you need to get rid of? Are there items that should be reserved for time alone only with your husband?

Before the day is over, talk through this topic with your husband. If necessary, make a drop off at a thrift store.

If you struggle in this area, ask God to help you.

Dear God,

Dare 31
Spectator Sport

☐ **Dare 31: Spectator Sport**

Proverbs 21:9
Better to live on a corner of the roof than share a house with a quarrelsome wife.

On one end of the continuum is a wife who is content to simply sit and enjoy her husband's company while he works on a project. On the other end of the continuum is a wife who nags, complains, and argues about seemingly trivial things. We all need to work a little harder at resting in the contentment that comes from simply enjoying our husband's company on his terms once in a while.

A Daughters Story...

Janice sat, legs crossed, sipping her coffee and fighting the urge to go inside. Her cookies waited; baking sheets, food coloring, and powdered sugar beckoned her from her kitchen. "You're wasting your time out here," one side of her brain stated.

"For some reason, this is valuable to him," the other side countered. The quiet battle went on in the recesses of her mind, but still she sat on the stool in her husband's workshop while he ran the belt sander over the wood. Occasionally Bob would look up at her and smile, then go back to his task.

"It's noisy out here," came the next thought.

"It's not a bad sound, reminds me of my dad's workshop," she countered. Three times he asked her to do something -

refreshing his coffee, finding a Phillips-head screwdriver, handing him his safety goggles. All drew but brief conversation from his lips. Her legs were getting a little stiff and her rear-end was falling asleep, but still she sat and watched.

Finally after an hour, he was done for the day. "Thanks for being out here with me, honey. I really enjoyed your company," he told her, smiling.

"No problem. I had a great time," she replied. What mystery of man had she uncovered? A very simple one indeed – her spouse, not unlike many men, spells love, "t–i–m–e." She thought of their three-year-old son who had spent the afternoon asleep while she "wasted" an hour watching her husband in his workshop. "Watch me, Mommy!" he would call to her repeatedly during the day. "Little boys grow into men who still want to be watched," she marveled.

Bottom Line: Sometimes marriage is a spectator sport – go shoulder to shoulder with your man and see how you build his esteem and how much he enjoys your company!

So What About You?

1) Are you focused on being productive, achieving results, or on the journey? Are you and your husband wired the same or different in this regard?

2) What does your husband enjoy doing with you? List 3 of his favorite activities:

a) _____
b) _____
c) _____

3) Choose one of these activities and schedule time to do it with him before the week is over. What are you doing and when?

4) What ONE thing can you do today to communicate to your husband that you are his number one fan? If you don't know, relate the story to him and ask him what would mean the most to him.

References to the "nagging wife" or "quarrelsome woman" are repeated five times in the book of Proverbs in the Bible. If you are feeling brave, ask your husband how you are doing in this area.

There's only one rule: You may not argue with him or justify any of your behavior.

You may only ask questions to clarify. If you are not ready to do this with him, ask an older child or a really good friend who sees you interact with your husband. Pray that God grows you in this area.

Dear God,

Dare 32
Crackle Paint

☐ **Dare 32:** Crackle Paint

Hebrews 10:24
And let us consider how we may spur one another on toward love and good deeds.

Too often we focus on our own needs and experience disappointment before we even have all the facts. A wise woman gathers information before responding to her circumstances.

A Daughters Story...

Reagan stared in disbelief as she watched her husband painting the antique bureau. White paint glared from the chipped corner, making the spot even more noticeable as it contrasted to the pale yellow with which the rest of the dresser was painted. Maybe she was wrong. Maybe that's primer he's painting on the spot. "Is that primer, honey?" she asked.

"No, it's paint. I got it this morning," he replied.

Reagan stood in the doorway of the bedroom, struggling with whether or not to say something else to him about it. Either he wouldn't see the problem or when he did figure it out, it would take two days to fix, depending on what he decided to do about it. He had promised to play tennis with her this afternoon and that might not happen if this project evolved into something major.

"Do you need something?" he asked, wondering why she was still standing there.

"No. Just saw you in here and thought I'd see how it was going," she replied. She remembered something one of the women in her *Daughters of Sarah* class said the week before about just being factual and not emotional during conversations with husbands. She really cared about going to tennis, not about how much time he spent on this project. "Will you be ready to leave for the courts in an hour? I have one reserved for 2pm." she calmly reminded him.

"Yeah, that should be good. Let me know about 20 minutes before we have to leave, so I can get ready, okay?" he replied.

Later, riding in the car on the way to play tennis, she asked him how it was going with the bureau. "I ran into a little trouble with the crackle paint technique, but I think I've got it worked out. I had to start over, but I think it will be pretty cool when I'm finished," he answered.

"Crackle paint? I thought you had decided against trying to do that with that piece," she replied.

"Yeah, I had. The more I thought about it, though, the more I decided you were right that the old bureau would look awesome with a crackle finish on it. I've never done it before, so it's going to take a bit of time. It's different than the other projects I've done. I think you'll like it when I'm finished, though," he responded.

"Wow, thanks, honey! I'm sure it will be just beautiful when you are finished," Reagan exclaimed. She realized that not only had she avoided an argument by not jumping to conclusions or being emotional. By just sticking to simple facts about what she wanted, she avoided an argument and created an opportunity to encourage him. Perhaps the best part was that she sensed the Holy Spirit had inspired her communication with him and nudged her gently in the direction she should go.

Bottom Line: Avoiding arguments and becoming more successful in your interactions with others. This comes from spending time in the Bible daily in order to discern the gentle and quiet voice of the Spirit within you.

So What About You?

1) Have you sensed the leading of the Spirit before? When? What was that like?

2) To clearly sense the Spirit, we have to spend time in prayer and spend time in the Bible on a daily basis. How are you doing in those two areas?

3) Take a few moments to look back at dares 1-10 and compare them to dares 20-30. If you measure progress *in terms of your desire to grow spiritually, instead of looking at external results,* what progress do you witness in yourself?

4) How have your motivations changed since the beginning of the dare?

5) As you look at your original vision and self-assessment from the beginning of the dare, even though there might still be room for improvement in those areas, what progress have you made? Make a list of all the things that are different about you now:

6) If you are in a small group, make a list of all the women in your group and how they are different:

7) Because your achievements will encourage others just like the Daughters stories have encouraged you, please consider sharing some of your successes, no matter how "small" with us at Information@greaterimpact.org. Even what you would consider a "small" blessing will encourage us and others, so please take a few moments to send us an email to let us know what is going on in your life.

Pray that God would help you want to live your life for Him. Ask Him to fill you with the desire to be pleasing to Him, to want to spend time with Him.

Pray that He give you pure motives.

Dear God,

Dare 33
Lights Out!

☐ **Dare 33: Lights Out!**

Hebrews 12:14
Make every effort to live in peace with all men and to be holy; without holiness no one will see the Lord.

Division of labor only works when both parties uphold their end of the bargain. For many women, the temptation to do what their husband has agreed to be responsible for is overwhelming and results in repeated rescuing and feelings of resentment. Wives who choose to trust their husband to keep his word, no matter what, do not get in God's way when He is trying to grow them both. One of the results of Eve's sin in the Garden of Eden is experienced by all women: the desire to control our husbands is strong. We must not succumb to this desire, lest we interfere with what God has planned.

A Daughters Story...

"I just feel betrayed!" Laura cried to Vera. "He won't listen to anyone, won't take advice, and won't be responsible! And now, once again, we almost had the power cut off. They canceled the cable and internet and they nearly canceled the insurance on the cars. This is like the sixth time the lady from the insurance agency has called me, wondering why we won't pay our bill. Why won't he pay them on time? It costs so much money to have all those things hooked up again, and I would just die of embarrassment if a neighbor asked why the power company truck was at our house! I just can't stand it. I thought I was getting a responsible guy when I married him, but all I've gotten is a man who would rather golf than pay our bills. So I keep asking him to deal with it, and he keeps promising he will, but then I finally end up doing it myself, and all the while I'm freaking out because I'm angry about him not handling it! I am so tired of having to do it all." Laura burst into tears after the words left her mouth.

Her older friend and mentor, Vera, put her arm around her and let her cry for a few moments. "I'm sorry you feel this way, honey. This is really hard for you, isn't it?" she quietly asked.

Calmer after her outburst, Laura replied, "I don't know what to do. I can't keep living this way. What do I do?"

Vera smiled at her younger friend. "I had some issues like this with Dick when we were first married," she began. "I remember one winter; he had been especially negligent in taking care of the power bill. We had three little kids at the time, Joey was still a baby. I remember feeling just like you do. When the third notice for the power bill showed up, I didn't cry or scream at him. I told him it was the last one they'd send before they shut off the power and I handed it to him. Well, we went for several days without power in the middle of winter because he just never got around to paying the bill. I'd like to say that was the only time it happened, but reality showed that it just wasn't. It's been twenty years since that happened, but he's a changed man. I'm thankful that God taught me to trust Him early, because I didn't feel compelled to nag him, even though I think he would have driven most other women crazy.

Laura, we're all the same. I'm dealing with diabetes and other health issues because I've refused to address my weight all these years. My husband, Dick, had to watch his children and wife shiver in the cold several times before he decided to take care of the bills promptly. I don't know what your issue is, but rest assured, honey, you probably have one! We all have areas of our lives where we are slow learners. But have hope! I've finally realized that God has grown Dick. I don't want you to have to wait thirty-five years to start seeing improvements in your marriage – but I can tell you that I had and still have as much learning to do as my husband. Now, I can see he's a real blessing."

Bottom Line: Stay out of God's way when He's teaching your spouse and just pray for him. Focus on what God wants to do in your life – focusing on another person's walk with God is pious, unproductive, and sure to make you miserable!

So What About You?

1) Have you ever gotten in God's way by rescuing your husband? When?

2) What about with your kids, if you have any? Where do you need to trust God more with them?

3) Did your parents let you learn lessons as a child or did they rescue you? How has that impacted your family relationships now?

4) Is there a situation in your life right now where you are getting in God's way of teaching your husband something?

5) What do you sense God teaching you through today's verse? Where do you need to be holy?

Today you may be greatly challenged. Or perhaps you are one of the few who is good at staying out of God's way. Today you get to pick from two questions, depending on which one would be the most challenging and beneficial for you to do:

1) Write down what you sense God is teaching your spouse that you sometimes prevent him from learning by rescuing him from consequences. Pray that God will enable you to stop interfering in this area and others if they exist.

   Or,

2) Write down what you sense God is trying to teach you that you are failing to really learn because either you are being rescued or the consequences have not become such that you are highly motivated to learn. Pray that God will enable things to change so you can grow in this area.

Dear God,

Dare 34
A Safe Place

☐ **Dare 34: A Safe Place**

Ephesians 4:31-32
Get rid of all bitterness, rage and anger, brawling and slander, along with every form of malice. Be kind and compassionate to one another, forgiving each other, just as in Christ God forgave you.

Our perceptions are often not correct. Only when we open ourselves up to the possibilities that we are wrong, can we truly grow and learn. Sometimes we need to simply listen and refrain from criticism or judgment.

A Daughters Story...

Tim walked in and set his computer backpack next to the table. Without saying a word, he hung up his coat, and sat down in his easy chair with the newspaper. He usually greeted his wife, Maxine, as she prepared dinner, but tonight the energy required for niceties and human connection completely escaped him.

Maxine, hearing him arrive and wondering where he was, came around the corner, wiping her hands on a dish towel. "Is something wrong?" she asked. For a moment, he just simply sat and stared at her. *Later she found out that this moment lasted so long because an internal war waged within his mind. His experiences in letting her know his frustrations in the past frequently ended up badly. She took things personally, even though they seldom had anything to do with her. So he sat and looked at her, debating whether or not to open up and confide in his wife.*

Finally, he spoke. "Things are bad with the business. I had to lay off six of our team today - all of them have been with me since we started the company. They understood, but I still feel bad about it. Financially, I'm uncertain as to how we're going to get through the next three months, even after laying people off."

Now it was her turn to stare at him. After a moment, she spoke. "Wow. I didn't know things were that bad. You've always taken good care of us, though, honey. We'll get through this, too. Do you want to talk about it?"

Gone were the insinuations of his lack of managerial skills, and this time no cutting remarks about his ineptness at dealing with people. Her tone was kind, gentle and compassionate. He took a risk and poured his heart out to her and all she did was listen this time. He found it a complete relief, and sensed that somewhere along the line, a burden had been lifted.

Maxine felt privileged to sit and listen to her husband's troubles. Her entire goal for the day was to not be critical, to be quick to listen, slow to speak and slow to become angry. While she now had some concerns about their financial situation, she realized that her husband was fully capable of dealing with it, and if he needed her assistance, he would ask. In the meantime, she would simply trust God and not worry about whether they would be taken care of or not.

Later, her husband told her that this conversation was a real turning point in their marriage - one that paved the way for deeper intimacy and greater trust between them.

Bottom Line: Be a safe place for your man to fall. When the entire world seems like it is out to get them, they'll come running home to you!

So What About You?

1) Does your husband consider you someone to whom he can safely confide?

2) The last time he confided in you, did you offer advice or did you simply listen?

3) How do you feel when your husband is upset about something? Do you take things personally when he is emotional?

4) Men often say that it's difficult for them to communicate any emotions. Are you feeling brave? Ask your husband if he is comfortable sharing his emotions with you. What does he say?

5) Is this different than what you previously thought? If so, how?

6) What can you do to be a woman who is a safe confidante for your man?

Your dare today is fairly challenging. You will do it in steps. Be careful to follow the directions, or it will not have the intended effect.

Take one piece of paper and draw a line down the middle, vertically. On the right side of the piece, write a list of all the things that your husband has done in the past or continues to do that frustrate you. After you have written an exhaustive list, look back to this box for the next step.

In the left column, write down how you typically respond to each of your husband's listed behaviors. When you have exhausted your responses, check back here for the next steps.

Take the paper and cut down the line, separating the sheet into a "his" side and a "her" side.

Take his side and burn it. Recognize that _you are not responsible_ for these behaviors of his, nor can you _directly_ impact them.

Spend 15 full minutes looking over the list of your own behavioral responses.

What do you see?

What do you sense God wants you to do with this experience?

Prayerfully thank God for what He has taught you through this exercise.

Commit to him what you are going to do differently as a result.

Dear God,

Dare 35
The Context

☐ **Dare 35: The Context**

Proverbs 18:2
A fool finds no pleasure in understanding, but delights in airing his own opinions.

Many women erroneously look toward marriage as the place where all their hopes and dreams will be fulfilled. Instead, we need to look at marriage as a context through which we grow more as a person. As we mature, we become less selfish and more giving. For those who have experienced motherhood, you have had to become less selfish about something even as simple as sleeping eight hours a night. When we get married, we have the opportunity to sacrificially love another adult. The immature adult thinks, "What can I get?" and the mature adult thinks, "What can I give?"

The Bible says a man is to love his wife as Christ loves the church, willing to sacrifice his life for her. Women are called to respect their husbands. While we don't often think of it this way, choosing respect can be a sacrificial decision, too.

A Daughters Story...

Terry, just finishing a long phone conversation with her mother, noticed that she still didn't have the breakfast or lunch dishes cleaned up. Now it was nearly time to make dinner. The baby had been sick, and after finally getting her down for a nap, Terry spent an hour watching her soap opera, trying to catch up on laundry and talk with her mom.

The phone was ringing again and it threatened to wake the baby, so she grabbed it. Her husband, Brian, needed her to run the tax folder up to his office fifteen minutes away. "I'm not going to do that. Yes, I know the appointment's tonight. No, I just don't have the time to do that – I haven't even brushed my hair or teeth yet today so I wasn't even planning on coming. You don't know what it's like to stay home with a crabby, sick baby all day. I'm busy beyond belief and exhausted. And my mother's having trouble with her landlord again and I need to help her figure that out." On and on she went, and finally, weary from the conversation, her husband let her know he needed to go, and hung up.

Unaware of their financial situation and how long it took to reschedule tax appointments, Terry was surprised when Brian walked through the door to pick up the documents. Had he really left work early to do come home and get them? What she also didn't know was that Brian's boss called him on the carpet earlier that same day for coming in late and leaving early. "Terry's having some difficulties adjusting to the new baby," he had told him. Unsympathetic to their family situation, his boss had simply replied, "I understand, but I recommend you figure it out, because it is becoming a performance issue."

Brian longed for the companionship he and his wife had enjoyed when she was working full time. She listened then. She seemed to have it together then. Now the entire universe revolved around the baby and Terry's emotional state at the moment. Too much drama filled his world now, and he simply didn't know what to do. But like a man, he squared his shoulders and just did the next thing. Unbeknownst to his wife, he was tired and just needed a friend. He loved five-month-old Jackie, and wouldn't trade her for anything, but really wished he hadn't become invisible as a result of her arrival. He had friends who had three and four kids – how did their wives do it? Yet another day passed without him feeling like he was needed for anything but the paycheck.

Bottom Line: Don't be so caught up in your own life that you forget to make your husband feel important today.

So What About You?

1) How often do you let your husband know how much you value his going to work every day? What do you do to communicate this?

2) How good a job are you doing to make your husband feel important? What is the most recent thing you've done to help him feel important?

3) Feeling brave? Ask your husband if he feels more important to you than anyone else (including kids, if you have them). What does he say?

4) Does most of your communication revolve around you and your activities or is it balanced with your husband's?

5) What one thing can you do today to help your husband feel important?

Think about this statement for a few moments:
Marriage is a context through which we have the opportunity to become more holy, not necessarily more happy.

God is more concerned with our holiness than our happiness. How does that concept fit into your thinking?

Your dare today is very simple. Make a list of things that are important to your husband. If you don't know what they are, ask him. Keep this list where you will see it every day and make a concerted effort to accomplish the list each week. Some of the items on your list might include, for example, keeping the van clean, having underwear in his drawer, doing something he enjoys with him, initiating sex, making his favorite meal, etc.

Pray God helps you accomplish this dare and gives you the energy and tenacity to achieve it weekly.

Things important to husband:

Dear God,

Dare 36
Sown in Tears

☐ **Dare 36: Sown in Tears**

Psalm 126:5-6
Those who sow in tears shall reap in joy. He who continually goes forth weeping, bearing seed for sowing, shall doubtless come again with rejoicing, bringing his sheaves with him.

God allows pain in our lives to shape us and build our reliance upon Him. Sometimes we wait until we are at the end of ourselves before we reach out to Him for help. The comfort that comes from walking with God is always available to us. Our job is just to recognize it and reach out to Him sooner, and we will suffer less.

A Daughters Story...

Alone and frightened, Juli felt the hard, cold steel on her legs as her feet rested in the stirrups. What she had hoped to be an encouraging appointment with her OB a week ago had degraded into a nightmare. After 18 months of fertility treatments mixed with five miscarriages, she was finally pregnant again and just knew God would let her carry this baby. Last week when she started spotting, she was sure it was just the fertilized egg attaching to the wall of the placenta, but then the bleeding became heavier and then two days ago, the pain started. Last week, the baby had a heartbeat. Today there was nothing.

"I'm sorry, Juli," the doctor said. After checking her, Dr. Sonjo told her, "There's a lot of clotting, and we've removed what we can for now. You need to walk around for two hours, come back and we'll check you again. If the pain returns significantly, don't wait, just come back to the office."

Juli wandered the hospital halls for about half an hour before the pain started again. By the time she hobbled back to Dr. Sonjo's office, she could barely stand. "We're going to do a D&C. That will clean out your uterus and hopefully put an end to the pain. Are you okay with that? You know the baby's gone, right?" asked Dr. Sonjo.

"Yes, I know. Do what you need to do," Juli responded. *What a lousy time for Bill to be in Memphis*, she thought.

Dr. Sonjo continued, "We can take care of this today if we just do a cervical block, and you'll be on your way home in an hour. However, this is going to be somewhat uncomfortable, so if you want anesthesia instead, we'll have to schedule it for tomorrow or the next day, based on what we have available."

"I just want to get this over with," Juli replied. Sitting in a strange metal chair, legs spread, she cringed when she saw the nurse bringing the needle for the block. "This is going to sting. Hold really still, I have to give you three injections," the nurse told her. A burning sensation crept through her, deep in her abdomen, then was gone. Two more times it returned. The nurse moved behind her and put her hands on Juli's shoulders as she explained the procedure.

Dr. Sonjo came in and began the D&C. Searing pain tore through Juli's abdomen as the suction pulled the matter from the inside of her uterus. She sat in the chair, trying to be brave. Never had she felt so alone. Silently, she repeated desperate prayers to the Lord, "Please, please...get it over soon."

Tears streamed down her face as she endured the harrowing pain. Several minutes later, just when she felt she could endure no more, it was all over. Juli wept with relief, signed out, made her co-pay, and let herself be driven home by her best friend.

Bottom Line: We are never alone when we choose to lean on God. He is always available, always awake, and always holds us up when we cannot stand on our own. Lean on Him and you can get through anything.

So What About You?

1) Do you know that God can handle your pain? When has He done this for you in the past?

2) Do you usually try to hold on to your pain or ask God to help you through it? Why have you responded that way?

3) What reference(s) can you find in the Bible that God can handle your pain?

4) How does today's verse impact you with regard to the pain you've endured in your own life?

After reading this, close your eyes and simply listen for God's voice, maybe even for as long as half an hour. Vividly imagine yourself in the most comfortable and safe room in your life today.

Sitting in a large chair in the corner of this room is a huge man, whom you recognize as the Lord. He's wearing a white pair of pants and a baggy short-sleeved white shirt. His features are chiseled with strength and he opens his arms to you. Crawling into his lap, you shrink in size until you are the size of a young child. His muscular arms envelope you as you rest your head on His chest. You are safe here. You can feel the warmth of His breath on your hair as He holds you.

"Daddy," you call Him.

"Daughter," He replies.

He is God. He loves you. He strokes your hair and you simply sit in His loving embrace, waiting for His words to come to you. After simply listening for a while, journal any truths revealed to you during this time on the next pages.

Pray for God to confirm anything He wants you to know or actions He wishes for you to take by communicating with you through circumstances, the Bible, or people over the next several days. Write those down. You may be challenged and forget what He has told you to do at a later time.

Notes from listening:

Dear God,

Dare 37
Just Go

☐ **Dare 37: Just Go**

1 Peter 2:5
You also, as living stones, are being built into a spiritual house, a holy priesthood, to offer up spiritual sacrifices acceptable to God through Jesus Christ.

A Daughters Story...

Standing in ICU holding her father's hand, Nina watched the heart monitors and waited. Tears slid silently down her mother's face as she watched her husband of 40 years die. "I'm so sorry, he's only got two or three more minutes," the doctor said when he called them into the room. The procedure which would either save him or kill him was over and his last breaths were being inhaled.

Suddenly, the monitors rose, startling everyone in the room. "It's adrenalin, his body's natural response," the nurse told them.

Twenty-five minutes and four adrenalin bursts later, an exasperated Nina asked the nurse, "Why is this happening?!"

"He has the heart and lungs of a 25-year-old man," came the reply.

Nina picked up a washrag and ran it over her father's ashen face. "Oh, Daddy, just go, it's okay, just go..." and as she glanced up at the monitors, they began to steadily drop. She looked at her mother, a rock of a woman who now seemed very frail. Her heart overflowed with compassion and sadness for this wife who had just lost her life partner. "Mom, I'm so sorry, I'm so sorry," Nina said, walking toward her mother, taking her in her arms, and holding her while they cried.

"What am I going to do? What am I going to do now?" Nina's mother repeated again and again. Stroking the back of her mother's hair, attempting to comfort her mom, Nina was surprised at the peace and lack of pain she herself felt.

Later, in looking back, she realized that it was the first time she could say that she was filled with the compassion of God. Literally absent were all the thoughts about her well-being and her own loss. She simply felt deep empathy and compassion for her mother and was concerned for her new circumstances as a widow.

Bottom Line: The more time you spend with God, the more you take on His character and His thoughts about what matters. True selflessness is a reflection of God's character and only comes as a result of time spent with Him.

So What About You?

1) Go back to the beginning of the book and review what you have written along the way. What stands out to you as the greatest challenge that you have overcome or made progress toward achieving?

2) What has been the most rewarding part of this journey for you so far?

3) Make a list of three areas where you sense you have behaved in a way that is pleasing to God:

   a. _____

   b. _____

   c. _____

4) Why do those areas please Him?

5) How do you feel about being pleasing to Him?

One of the few ways we can offer love back to God is by obeying Him. Your challenge today is to deeply pray for a heart that yearns to be pleasing to God and ask Him for His assistance with your obedience. John 14:23a says, "Those who love me obey my teaching."

Now read Chapter 28 of Deuteronomy in the Bible, which describes the many blessings for those who obey, and demonstrates the fact that disobedience results in consequences.

Ask God for clarity in understanding why there are consequences for poor choices if He is a good and just God.

Ask Him to relate this to your marriage.

Write down what He causes you to sense.

Thank Him for the insight.

Insights:

Dear God,

Dare 38
Initiate

☐ **Dare 38: Initiate**

1 Peter 2:2-3
You've had a taste of God. Now, like infants at the breast, drink deep of God's pure kindness. Then you'll grow up mature and whole in God.

If we have children, we want them to trust us because we know vastly more than they do about the consequences of their choices. We want what is best for them, and therefore steer them toward choices that will facilitate beneficial outcomes. God does this for us as well. He is kind. He wants what is best for us. We just need to trust Him and remember that He has our best interests at heart. The more we trust God, the more mature and whole we become.

A Daughters Story...

Linda lay in bed, listening to her husband close up the house for the night. Larry's day had been excessively difficult, and she knew he was more than ready for some sleep. She also sensed that lovemaking would seriously distract him from his challenging day, in a very good way.

The problem, however, was the same one they'd dealt with their entire marriage. Linda was one of the 50% of women who have "low sex drive." Like many other women, she did not experience physical arousal until she and her husband had been engaged in intimacy for about ten minutes. But for whatever reason, she still hesitated when it came to initiating sex with her husband.

Mike's footsteps thumped up the hardwood steps to the second floor. "Initiate…" she thought. She heard her husband opening the doors to the children's rooms, checking on them, and then wandering down the hall again. "It's now or never…" she thought again. She smiled at her husband when he walked into their bedroom. "Lock the door," she said. He stopped, looked at her, and raised an eyebrow. About ten minutes later, she thought, "Oh, I remember now…how could I keep forgetting that I like this?"

Like many women who are only intimate on an intentional basis, she decided to put more effort into the frequency and creativity behind the locked door. Her husband didn't say anything to her about the increased intimacy, but oddly enough, she did notice he was getting more of his household chores done. When her van ended up in the shop for a week, he gave her his car to drive and he drove the old truck to the office.

While online once, she found a challenge by Michelle Weiner-Davis, the author of several books on intimacy, that dared wives to initiate lovemaking and see what happened at home. She decided to take this challenge herself as well, and found it expressed respect to her husband.

Bottom Line: Initiating sex communicates respect in a unique and special way to our husbands. When our husbands feel desired by us, their esteem is built, thus enabling them to fully and confidently engage in their roles as men.

So What About You?

1) Are you comfortable initiating sex with your husband? Why or why not?

2) Have you ever initiated sex? When was the last time?

3) If you have initiated sex in the past, how did your husband respond?

4) Why do you think you don't initiate sex more frequently?

5) Knowing what God has to say about this, and recognizing that it is a complex issue for many women, what is the very least you can do to grow in this area?

6) What would indicate that you have made improvements in this area?

Today, pray that God helps you overcome any obstacles that stand in the way of physical intimacy for you and your spouse. Pray that God not only heal you of any past issues you might have, but that He also takes your physical relationship with your husband to a new level. Challenge yourself to initiate, especially if prompted by the Spirit!

Dear God,

Dare 39
Caroline's Father

☐ Dare 39: Caroline's Father

Matthew 6:14
For if you forgive men when they sin against you, your heavenly Father will also forgive you.

So often we think there is only one way of looking at things. We think we know what is real and what is true. God's perspective is often different than ours; sometimes even dramatically so.

A Daughters Story...

Caroline stared at her mother in the abortion clinic. "This is your own fault," her mother accused and looked away.

The curt remark seared what remained of sixteen year old Caroline's heart. Her mother's husband (she could no longer call him her father) had repeatedly sexually molested her for the last six years of her life. Consequences in the form of a young life growing inside her stole what remained of her innocence as she and her mother waited in the lobby of the abortion clinic. Desperate and bereft for a mother's comfort, aching to be a mother herself and not wanting to end the life of her child, Caroline simply sat frozen, shocked and afraid.

She understood her mother's anger. Encouraged by a good friend, Caroline had shared her situation with a school counselor, and the police arrived on their front step that afternoon. That was a week ago, and her mother's anger had only grown. Caroline's reprieve from the smell and sweat of the man who only disgusted her had also had an unexpected and painful result. Instead of standing by her daughter, her mother was embarrassed and angry. Acting out of her warped thinking, she told Caroline and her siblings that it was Caroline who had "dishonored and disgraced the family name." Caroline was angry, too. She regretted sharing the truth.

The death of the unborn baby only added to the anger and pain that seethed inside Caroline for many years. Nightmares haunted her sleep, and feelings of grief and unworthiness saturated her soul. Incarcerated, her father had ceased communication with nearly everyone in her family. They had all moved on in their own lives until his release. What astounded her was that her own brother, mother, and aunt still held grudges against her, as if she were truly responsible for their losing their own father, husband, and brother for the seven years he spent in prison. Therapy had helped Caroline some, but one day, she found herself staring at herself in the bathroom mirror and realized that she was exhausted from carrying all the pain and anger around with her. Having been raised in a church-going family, she had walked away from her faith as a result of what had happened to her. How could a so-called Christian do this to his daughter? How could a Christian mother respond so poorly? Caroline had nearly decided God Himself didn't exist. But today, in the mirror, she saw a lonely woman aged with grief, who sabotaged relationships to prevent anyone from knowing her well enough to hurt her. She missed Danny, the most recent man from whom she had walked away. He was truly husband material, and she thought she had fallen in love with him, but her fear, stronger than her loneliness, won out.

The lump began in Caroline's throat and continued to grow until it emerged as a sob. Wrought with grief, Caroline's body slumped to the floor of the bathroom and she wept as though a floodgate in her soul had been opened. Sobs wracking her body, she gave in to the pain, the fear, the anger, letting all the emotion wash over her. At the heart of all of it was the ache of loneliness. "How long, God, how long will I hurt? Where have You been? Why aren't You there?" she cried. Finally spent, lying on the tile floor of the bathroom, Caroline prayed. "God, if You're out there, I think I need You. I want to stop feeling like this." She arose and walked into her bedroom where she kept a Bible. She opened it in the hopes that something would speak to her, and her eyes fell on Matthew 6:14.

"Forgive him?" she thought, thinking of her father.

"Forgive me?" she also thought, remembering the abortion.

An image of Jesus filled her mind. She realized that every tear she had cried, He wiped away.

An image of Jesus on the cross emerged in her mind – a new awareness of the meaning behind the gift of Christ. Yes, they had talked about that in her childhood Sunday school classes, but it never had much meaning – just religious words. Now she understood. God's son, like her, had been treated unfairly. Beaten and tortured, spat upon and hammered to a cross, she realized that her pain and the pain Christ went through were similar. Christ had felt alone, just as she often did. And God offered this man, His own son, as payment for her sins as well as anyone else who wanted to go to heaven. If she remembered right, all she needed to do was accept the gift. Caroline was sure she had done this as a child at church. One thing remained for her now, however, and that was forgiveness. She saw something she'd never before seen in the crucifixion – God offered this "gift" because He wanted to forgive us, wanted to forgive her.

She also saw God wanted her to forgive her father.

"I can't do this on my own," she prayed. "Help me forgive him. I don't know how much I mean this, but okay, I forgive him. I forgive him and I ask You to do whatever you want with him, but as for me, I will be done hating him. And You know there's not a day that goes by that I don't think of the baby. You know I wish I had run out of that clinic. I'm so sorry! God, please forgive me – I didn't know, I …" and the words were replaced with sobs as Caroline dissolved into tears again.

When she felt she could cry no more, a sense of peace and warmth saturated Caroline's heart. She simply sat, overwhelmed by the experience for a few moments. Over the course of the next week, she found herself sitting at her kitchen table, writing a letter to her father and mother, letting them know how she had hurt over the years, but also communicating the forgiveness she now honestly felt as her own. As the weeks passed, she found herself more at peace than she had ever been in her life, replacing the hate that had permeated her being for so long.

Somewhere in the midst of the release, she called Danny. Two years later they were married and now celebrate life together while raising a family of their own.

Bottom Line: Forgiveness is a concept that moves one forward in his or her faith like nothing else does. God is an expert on forgiveness because of His own experience with Jesus. "Forgive and you will be forgiven," makes sense only once you understand the concept from God's perspective.

So What About You?

1) How did today's Daughters story affect you?

2) Where in your life have you struggled or still struggle with the concept of forgiveness?

3) How has lack of forgiveness robbed you or your family?

4) Why is it sometimes easier to hold on to hate than to experience the release of forgiveness?

F

Forgiveness has many layers and is worthy of study. Today, do a search in your Bible and online on the topic of "forgiveness." Pray that God helps you to overcome any obstacles that stand in the way of forgiveness for you or for someone else. Know that God wants you to forgive others and He wants to forgive you. Trust Him in this and take action toward forgiveness today.

Dear God,

Dare 40
Your Story!

☐ **Dare 40: Your Story!**

Psalm 111:10
The fear of the Lord is the beginning of wisdom; a good understanding have all that do his commandments; his praise endures forever.

You have been through much in the last 39 dares!

Hopefully, you have become wiser and gained understanding as you have experienced *The Respect Dare.*

Congratulations on making it this far! Today, you write your own story, an example of a time when one of the Scriptures used over the last 39 dares came to life inside the context of your own marriage. Write a short story, describing a single incident that means the most to you as evidence of God's work in your life. Start with the following in the first sentence:

1. Who was there
2. When it happened
3. Where you were

And then tell the "what" of the incident. End with your own bottom line statement that gives advice to someone else. Be prepared to share this story with a friend, your small group, or your husband.

Your Story:

Feeling brave? Share your story with us at
Information@greaterimpact.org for possible publication
in our next book!

The following prayer is based upon the psalms and other scriptures in the Bible. Your dare today involves listening in two different situations:

1) As you pray, be open to sensing what the Spirit would have you learn. This dare is all about your own story, your own journey, your own experience with God's guidance. Spend 20-30 minutes listening and dwelling in the words, writing down anything you sense is important.

2) Spend some time today listening to inspirational music. Ask God to speak to you through the lyrics and follow any inclinations you have. Listen for about an hour.

Oh Lord Most High, Creator of all things, Redeemer, Conqueror!

I praise You. I worship only You. Thank You for watching over me and everyone I hold dear. Thank You for my marriage. Thank You for this relationship which can grow me in Your ways and Your sight. I have trouble understanding Your ways; they are a mystery. But I will trust in Your sovereignty and believe in Your faithfulness. I want to know You more.

Father, help me be a wise woman. Help me be beautiful in Your sight. Create in me a new life, oh Lord, that I may be a new creation to better worship, and serve Your purposes and not my own. Help me have an eternal perspective of marriage. Help me see it as but another opportunity to follow You and become holy. Enable me to spend time in Your Word and talk with You daily. I desire wisdom, Father. I yearn to be pleasing in Your sight. I confess I have not been obedient as a wife and a woman of faith, and I have fallen short. Teach me, oh Lord. Show me where I can grow. Help me be a woman of strength and dignity, laughing at the days to come. Fan in me the flames of courage and enable me to obey Your Word. I praise Your name and thank You for the blessings in the days to come! May they all be for Your glory!

What's Important:

Dare 41
New Beginning

☐ **Dare 41: New Beginning**

Philippians 1:6
And I am sure that God, who began the good work within you, will continue His work until it is finally finished on that day when Christ Jesus comes back again.

Today, spend 20-30 minutes reading through the pages of this book, paying attention to the notes you made along the way, the questions you answered, and the prayers you wrote. Highlight or underline the prayers that God has answered.

Today is the day you review your list of expectations for your own behavior changes that you made on Dare 1, and answer the following questions:

1) Were the expectations I had of myself realistic?

2) What progress have I made on these expectations?

3) Do I need to adjust my expectations of myself or my husband? Why or why not?

4) Review the initial assessment you took back on Day 3 and circle any areas where you have seen progress. Pray that God helps you see the truth, and not be discouraged. Remember, any effort is going to result in improvements! What did you discover?

5) Sit down with your husband and go over the assessment with him, and ask him where he has seen improvement in you over the last 40 dares. Pray that God helps you both see the truth. If your husband does not see the same changes you have, without becoming defensive, explain to him what you have been doing that is different, and ask him to comment. What did you discover?

6) Where have you grown in the following areas, compared to where you were when you started *The Respect Dare?*

Disciple

Household Manager

Communicator

Confident and Assured Woman

Revisit the purpose statement you created that you have been reading every single day for the last 40 days. On this and the next page, incorporating the previous assessment and everything else you've learned, write a new, positive tensed, "I am" vision statement for yourself. Refer back to the original instructions if you have questions.

After completing this statement, tape it somewhere you will see it more than once daily.

Pray for God to complete this work within you. Share it with your group and ask them to pray for you.

Purpose Statement:

Dear God,

Your final dare is simple, but a little risky.

Today, call several girlfriends who are not in your current respect dare group. Schedule a coffee with them.

Tell them about your experience with *The Respect Dare* and invite them to join you in starting a new group of dare-takers. Lead, pray, and support them through the 40-dare process to not only help other women grow in their marriages and spiritually, but to continue your own growth. Join our Facebook® page by searching "The Respect Dare" and be part of our community of growth!

If you want to utilize some of our methods, please know we have an inexpensive small group guide available at Amazon.com and other retailers.

May God be with you and may your experience glorify Him and multiply in more marriages!

Love to you,
Nina

Visit us at http://www.greaterimpact.org for more resources and free marriage tips!

End Notes

1   Contemporaryfamilies.org, "Council on
    Contemporary Families, CCF Briefing Paper: New
    Findings on Women's Earnings and Housework,"
    September 4. 2007,
    http://www.contemporaryfamilies.org/
    subtemplate.php?t=briefingPapers&ext=
    womenshousework> (March 3, 2009).
2   World Bank.org. "Where is the Wealth of Nations?
    Measuring Capital for the 21st Century," 2006. The
    International Bank for Reconstruction and
    Development/The World Bank,
    <http://siteresources.worldbank.org/
    INTEEI/214578-1110886258964/20748034/All.pdf>
    (February 2, 2009).
3   Feldhahn, Shaunti, *For Women Only: What you
    need to know about the inner lives of men*. (Sisters,
    Oregon; Multnomah Publishing, a division of
    Random House, 2005), 77.
4   John LaRue, Jr. , "The Internet: Blessing or Curse
    for Pastors?" March 1, 2001,
    <http://www.christianitytoday.com/yc/2001/mara
    pr/18.88.html> (December 17, 2008).
5   Feldhahn, 113.

About The Author

Nina has seen God's hand at work in the courses He's inspired her to write. Over 95 percent of her participants report improving their relationship with God and becoming more confident. She firmly believes that to be fully productive and have peace, one must live life for the Audience of One, being fully engaged in all the roles He has placed us in. She has found her calling in leaving secular business to write and deliver courses and retreats for Christians at a fraction of the cost of what the same high caliber of training goes for in the marketplace.

Nina has over 20 years in the communications and training industry including 15 years with the largest and most successful training company in the world. She has coached numerous executives and pastors around the country and currently provides leadership for Greater Impact Ministries, Inc. as Executive Director.

Nina's expertise in the classroom as a facilitator, trainer, and coach display her God given talents. The ministry has recently taken steps to provide Daughters of Sarah® to churches around the nation, via video, keeping with Nina and her husband, Jim's goals of raising their family together. They met in 1985 and married in 1991 after Nina finished her Masters degree at West Virginia University. She and Jim are privileged to be raising their 3 children, Adam, Bram, and Elizabeth, together in Loveland, Ohio. Though her available dates are relatively few, as her family is her primary concern, Nina can be booked for speaking engagements, courses, or retreats through the ministry website at http://www.greaterimpact.org .

There is more.

Have you ever wondered, "Isn't there more?"
Like something is missing?

There is.

We can help you find it. That's what we're all about.
You're not meant to do this on your own. God created us
to rely on Him, but we don't. We fight it. We think we can
do it by ourselves and that maybe God will be proud of us
when we figure it out.

**Here's the truth: He wants to do it with us. Through us.
He has a plan for each of us.**

Join us and receive training, teaching, and knowledge that
will change how you live your life. We listen and offer
feedback, and celebrate with you as God does truly big
stuff. **With Him, you can make a greater impact**. In your
marriage. With your children. At your workplace.

Join us and discover your more.
1. Retreats
2. Workshops
3. Courses

Redefining training to redefine lives.
554 Belle Meade Farm Drive * Loveland, Ohio 45140 *
513.310.6019 * www.greaterimpact.org

Small Group Leader's Guide

This book is written such that the questions are ones that can easily be used in small groups without a great deal of preparation on your part, as long as you are comfortable with the content and women's struggles. We suggest combining a small group experience with the E-Course offered for a very small fee at http://www.greaterimpact.org , or purchasing the small group guide from http://www.Amazon.com . The E-Course will provide video teaching segments that you can play at your meeting once a week for eight weeks to complete the dares as a group, and supply you with additional resources. You can also sign up for a private group if you have a minimum of ten participants. Only do five dares a week if doing this in a group. When facilitating a small group, keep these things in mind:

1. Stress confidentiality to all your group members every single week. Make it the first thing you do when you get together. You might say something like, "We want to have an environment where we can be transparent and share, so our one rule is that whatever is shared here, stays here. You are encouraged to talk about what we're doing, but do it in a way that doesn't identify any specific individual." Reminding them of the confidentiality in this way allows them to talk things over with their spouse, a sister, or other friend, but also protects the identity of the group members.

2. You should open each session with a short prayer, inviting God to be present and lead your discussion. You should also feel the freedom to pray for individuals as the session is going on if someone is extremely upset about a situation, etc.

3. Do not offer advice, but rather turn the women in your group back to God's advice. If someone is asking what she should do about something, then encourage discussion about what the Bible says, rather than allowing the women to offer a bunch of opinions. Have a concordance handy or a topical index so you can look things up rather quickly if need be.

4. Don't put anyone on the spot when asking the questions. You might even consider beginning by asking something non-threatening like, "What did you think of the dares for this week?"

5. Don't go around the table or room for input. Instead, allow women to contribute as they feel led. Be careful not to put someone on the spot.

6. Ask open ended questions, rather than questions that end with, "Yes," or "No."

7. At the end of your meeting time, ask for prayer requests for the women to pray over between meetings. It is okay to go around the room at this time.

8. Be transparent as a leader, but be careful not to monopolize the time talking about yourself. It takes at least six seconds for the human brain to respond to a question, so wait a bit before jumping in with your own examples or responses. If you start answering first early on in the meetings, your group will expect you to do this each week and then will not share as easily.

9. Be in prayer about each of the women in between meetings, and have a friend or two pray for you specifically while you are leading your group.

If you have questions, please feel free to email us at Information@greaterimpact.org .

Be sure to join our Facebook® page and continue your growth by searching "The Respect Dare."

Made in the USA
Lexington, KY
08 April 2012